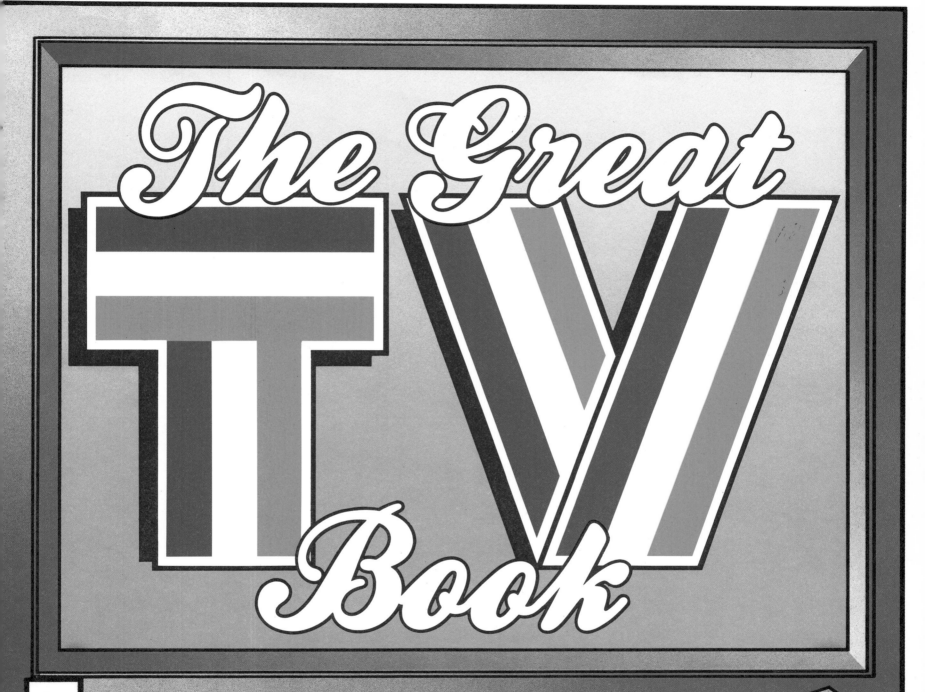

The Great TV Book

21 YEARS OF LWT

EDWARD DURHAM TAYLOR

SIDGWICK & JACKSON

LONDON

First published in 1989
by Sidgwick & Jackson Limited

Copyright © 1989 by
London Weekend Television

Designed by
Grub Street Design, London.

ISBN 0–283–99923–3

Printed in Great Britain
by Eagle Press
for Sidgwick & Jackson Limited
1 Tavistock Chambers
Bloomsbury Way
London WC1A 2SG

Contents

Piece of Cake
featured dare-devil young
pilots during the first year of
the Second World War. Playing
them were Boyd Caines, Tim
Woodward, Neil Dudgeon,
George Anton, Tom Burlinson
and Nathaniel Parker
★

PART ONE

Holding us spellbound with top-class drama

'IT WAS POURING rain most of the time and we were knee-deep in mud pretending that it was a nice sunny day. It wasn't easy.' Actor John Alderton is talking about filming *Forever Green*. 'There were a lot of problems shooting in that cottage with its small rooms and rather a large crew. We all had to be on our best behaviour, otherwise tempers could very easily get frayed. The irony was that someone phoned while the series was on and asked why it never rained in the place where we lived in the series.'

The programme was a big hit with viewers, attracting over 15 million of them on Sunday nights. John Alderton and LWT seem to go well together – first with the comedy *Please Sir* in 1968, then the all-time favourite, *Upstairs, Downstairs* with both John and his wife Pauline Collins and this year with *Forever Green* (once again with John and Pauline as co-stars), the series that put green issues on our screens – matters such as the environment, conservation and alternative medicine.

From being a young repertory actor in 1962, John became a television actor for the first time in ATV's *Emergency Ward 10*. 'To be able to learn the craft of television acting in a twice-weekly serial like that was hard for a young actor but the best possible training course – you just had to learn quickly.

'It is gratifying to have another series again that pulls such high viewing figures I must admit.'

While he was filming *Forever Green* he was also appearing in *Waiting for Godot* at the National Theatre, hence the beard and the short hair which have given him a new look for viewers. 'Perhaps because I wasn't known as a "green" – although I am interested in all those issues – my character as a doubter turning greener gained credibility.'

Forever Green followed close on the heels of another big Sunday success, *Wish Me Luck*. Drama series set in wartime have always been popular; they provide wonderful stories of human interest. For actress Kate Buffery, *Wish Me Luck* must have seemed like an adventure story. Yet for many viewers the war is remembered as a very real time in their lives. Had she any qualms about the part?

'Well, there are two sides to that. First, we were making a drama not a documentary and we were trying to appeal to and entertain a wide audience. But I was, and am still, wary of what we were doing because there are such Resistance people as I played still alive – I met some of them – and there is no way you can compare with them. You just try to glean bits of information that will help you in a part like that. The truth, however, could have been very different. Some of the Resistance people I met said the work could be very boring sometimes because there was a lot of waiting around doing nothing. So I listened to them and found that the more I learned the more interested and involved I became.'

Were any of her own family in the war? 'My father was in a tank regiment out in India and I asked him about his feelings then, just to add to my own sense of what the war as a whole must have been like.'

After ten years husband and wife team John Alderton and Pauline Collins were back acting together in 1989 in LWT's Sunday night series *Forever Green*. It illustrated people's concerns for the quality of life and for the environment. While many of its 15 million viewers may – like John – never have been a committed 'green', most will have been caught up in the issues the series raised about our more hectic and stressed society

★

Could she personally have done what Liz Grainger did in *Wish Me Luck* – leave her family and go to France – when it was known during the war that many of the undertakings of the Resistance ended in death or capture? 'Knowing what I know now, I couldn't have done it. Such people had an extraordinary quality about them and were very single-minded about what they were doing.'

What was the most difficult part of it? 'Some of the scenes which you thought might be difficult weren't. For example, killing a person is not beyond our comprehension and imagination; we must all have wondered about it at some time. There were scenes where the motivation was difficult to get right because these people were so unusual in character and not always heroic or even likeable.'

She enjoyed the glamorous side of playing a part in that era. 'The details of the costumes were fascinating, and the way women in particular would make do and mend in order to look attractive and at their best. Having my hair in curlers wasn't all that fascinating – I wouldn't like to do that every night!'

Thirteen million viewers used to watch *We'll Meet Again* (1982) in which Susannah York played a World War II doctor and wife whose husband was serving in Europe and invalided out paralysed. The American Air Force arrives at an airfield near the quiet market town where she lives. The story revolves round the friction and attraction between the villagers and their new 'guests' and the relationships that are formed. Michael J. Shannon played the American major and former playboy whose job was to smooth relations with the community. He falls for the attractive doctor and she for him.

'I liked the way it was cast and the great attention to detail,' says Susannah York. 'Before I started work on it I tried to get the feel of what those times were like by talking to a lot of older people who remember the war years well. And of course I had seen a lot of old black and white films and been in war films before. Great care was taken with everything and it was very strong on production values. I do remember getting a lot of mail from a whole range of people – children, young people, old people.'

The series was shot in Kent. 'One night when we were down on a beach

COUNTDOWN TO THE SCREENING

How long do drama series take to make? From plotting the storylines to the series appearing on the screen takes about fifteen months.

Wish Me Luck, which will return next year, is a good example. Last autumn storylines were commissioned. They are very important because what is in the story-line is often decisive in determining how much money is spent. If the stories were all set in France the costs would be very high, so stories have to include some London sequences. The scripts were written in the spring. The 'recce' for suitable locations was done while the second series was being edited, and by then casting and design were under way as well. Shooting started in June in France and will go on intermittently till November. Editing each episode will go on while the next ones are being made. The whole series will be ready for showing in January.

Not much rehearsal is done for film drama, whereas in the old days, when it was all done with cameras in the studio, performances were rehearsed and polished in the rehearsal rooms to be ready for studio and camera. Nowadays, for film drama, each scene is normally rehearsed with the director on the set, and then there is usually a long gap while the technicians are setting up what the director and actors have decided will work best.

ABOVE LEFT
**Kate Buffery
learned a lot about how a
drama series comes about in
*Wish Me Luck***
★

filming a love scene with me and Michael, one of the crew called a warning to us because a man had started to throw rotten cabbages at us. He obviously thought what we were doing had no place in his little corner of England,' says Susannah.

That distinguished and thoughtful actor, Peter Barkworth, was one of the stars of an earlier war series, *Manhunt*, in 1970. It was the story of an RAF pilot, played by Alfred Lynch, who was forced to parachute into occupied France and helped by the local Resistance group. It was filmed at Burnham Beeches in Buckinghamshire because the team found roads there unmarked by white or yellow lines and because the attractive countryside could have been France. Unfortunately, it was also on a flight path to Heathrow.

Peter Barkworth played an English-man who lived in France and had become the leader of the group. Actress Cyd Hayman was one attractive member of it. Peter enjoyed the part but remembers the production as a 'sticky' one. 'We were using a multi-camera technique, which was all right in the studio, but made outside filming difficult. We often had to wait for clear skies and the cameras to be set up. Then a lot of the scenes were long and because they were, we were often at the mercy of planes flying over – when of course we had to stop filming.

'Cyd Hayman was a godsend to all of us because she lightened the atmosphere so well. What I didn't like was rehearsing the fight scene with Alfred Lynch. We had to make it as realistic as possible and I loathed going to rehearse that.

WRITER'S REWARD

How much do writers get paid? It can vary – from £4,000 to £250,000. They are paid differently for different jobs, such as an original story, an adaptation or an episode of a series. If they have no record in television, and are being asked to write a script to an agreed storyline for an existing series, they might be offered £4,000. An experienced, successful writer would get double that. Scripts for films are different. They could earn a writer £20,000, which is cheap, or £250,000, which is exceptional.

Most writers will take a month to write an hour of drama. They get 'residuals' – repeat fees – for it as well as the original fee. Television writers don't starve; the prolific ones do very nicely, thank you. When most drama costs between £400,000 and £500,000 an hour, and some £1 million, the payment for the script seems small – but of course it's only one part of what goes into a production for the screen.

Maureen Lipman in the very funny cricket play *Outside Edge*

★

'Robert Hardy joined the series playing a German sergeant and all of a sudden we started to get more attention from the critics. I thought he gave a great bravura performance, although I think there was some resentment that after we had been going for some ten episodes or so he seemed to come along and almost steal the show. But his part simply contrasted with what we had to do.'

●

DÉBUT OF A BESTSELLER

Frederick Forsyth, author of such blockbusters as *The Odessa File* and *The Day of the Jackal*, will see his first television films on the screen this autumn. He formed his own company

SINGLES CHAMPIONS

All the talk now is of independents as television pioneers, but the pioneering actually started twenty-one years ago when a group of outstanding drama producers, directors and writers formed Kestrel Productions. LWT hired them to make films and plays and they sought out the country's best writers.

One of the very first was Dennis Potter, now regarded as television's outstanding drama writer. This controversial writer who was to go on to write *Pennies from Heaven*, which starred Bob Hoskins and Cheryl Campbell, and *The Singing Detective*, with those awful pictures of Michael Gambon as a sufferer from a terrible skin disease, provided a story in 1968 called *Moonlight On the Highway*. Starring Ian Holm, this was about a loner who runs a society dedicated to the 1930s singer Al Bowlly.

Martin Shaw, the crooner-seducer in *Cream In My Coffee*

The play was directed by one of the few really legendary figures of British television, James MacTaggart, who sadly died in 1974.

Dennis Potter returned to LWT in 1980 to make six single dramas. Two years later, one of the six, *Cream In My Coffee*, with Peggy Ashcroft, Lionel Jeffries and Martin Shaw, won the most important television prize in Europe, the Prix Italia. Martin Shaw, who played the forty-year-old crooner with the orchestra at a luxurious resort hotel, remembers it well. 'What is there to say? It was inevitable with such a writer and cast, combined with a great director, Gavin Millar,

Colin Welland, writer and star of *Bangelstein's Boys*

and a producer, Kenith Trodd, who always fights for the money to make drama to the highest standard.' Martin Shaw is now concerned that in the current commercial climate there won't be as many opportunities to make drama of that quality.

A young actor from BBC's *Z Cars*, Colin Welland, turned writer in the late 1960s and the result was a Kestrel film for LWT, its first, *Bangelstein's Boys*. Welland also played one of the leads in this true-to-life story of a rugby club's excursion to a big game. The script's use of four-letter words gave the company its first brush with censorship. The writer, who went on to win an Oscar for the 1981 film *Chariots of Fire*, was on his way – and P.C. Graham no longer patrolled in a Z Car.

Taking a swipe at the IBA's way of awarding ITV franchises was the theme of Nemone Lethbridge's *The Franchise Trail* (1968), which was planned as LWT's opening play. On reflection, however, cocking a snook at the IBA on the company's first weekend on air seemed a bit cheeky and the showing was postponed for a few weeks.

Alan Bennett wrote a series of acclaimed single dramas for LWT, including *Me, I'm Afraid of Virginia Woolf*, *One Fine Day* and *Afternoon Off*.

Colin Firth, one of the schoolboys learning about life in *Dutch Girls*

Through the drawing together of television and film interests, LWT has made single films such as *Blue Money*, *Outside Edge*, *Dutch Girls* and Evelyn Waugh's *Scoop*. Another Waugh story, *A Handful of Dust*, has been made into a very successful feature film. Derek Granger and Charles Sturridge who made it are the team who made Waugh's *Brideshead Revisited* into one of the most celebrated serials in world television.

Though the spirit and devotion to making top-class drama for television has remained the same, crucial factors have changed almost beyond belief: £40,000 was a typical outlay for a single drama in 1968 – £2 million is a likely outlay for a 1989 television film drama.

John Thaw, who has
had a big success as Inspector
Morse, played a Fleet Street
crime reporter in LWT's 1984
series *Mitch*

★

Frank Finlay won a
BAFTA award for his
portrayal of the Fuehrer in the
1973 play *The Death of Adolph
Hitler*. Frank recalls, 'I very
rarely watch myself on
television but I did in fact see
this production, and I have to
admit that I forgot I was
playing the leading role'

★

Peter Vaughan with his distinctive features seemed ideally cast as the relentless detective pursuing the **Mr Big** and his gang who got away with a huge haul of gold bullion in the 1969 success *The Gold Robbers*

★

A B O V E   R I G H T
The Gentle Touch was a big break for Jill Gascoine, seen here with William Marlowe. She remembers the long-running series as a hard slog made easier because of having a very friendly team

★

R I G H T
Poirot – the clever and fastidious Agatha Christie detective. David Suchet seemed to capture more what the writer had in mind than the somewhat comic creations of other actors

★

FFS – in 1987 with Murray Smith, a well-known writer of ITV series, to produce six films from new stories he has written. It is unusual these days for new television groups to be led by writers but it is a move many will welcome.

Freddie actually hasn't written the scripts himself. 'I did write a screenplay once – the film wasn't made in the end. But I decided that scripting was a different craft from writing continuous prose and novels. I am a good watcher,' says Freddie, 'and Murray is a good listener and can write excellent dialogue. So I mapped out the twenty- to thirty-page storylines and Murray developed them into drama scripts for one-and-three-quarter hour slots.'

Freddie will be story editor as well as executive producer on all six films, which include plots about espionage, arms-running and assassination. He was looking for a high level of authenticity in the casting. 'The Germans are being played by German actors, the British by British, the Americans by Americans.

'We have had a handsome budget and first-class, experienced international directors,' says Freddie. 'I think it is very exciting because I have gradually been moving towards being involved in television. It is a huge international market and international co-production will just go on increasing. There is money now being spent on television films just as it used to be on cinema films.'

•

DETECTING THE WINNERS

Cops and robbers series have always provided enjoyment for viewers because they have satisfying, shapely stories and inbuilt drama with plenty of human interest angles to pursue.

One of LWT's early successes was *The Gold Robbers*, a thirteen-part story starring Peter Vaughan as a policeman investigating a massive gold bullion robbery. Other stars in the series included Ian Hendry, Bernard Hepton, George Cole and Roy Dotrice. The series followed Peter Vaughan's search for the thieves and looked at how the robbery had affected their lives. Mr Big (played by Richard Leech) was revealed at the end. The robbery was actually staged at an airfield near Camberley in Surrey.

Peter Vaughan, whose striking features are instantly recognizable through many years of television and cinema roles, says, 'ITV ratings weren't doing very well at the time, I remember, and *The Gold Robbers* began on a Friday night and went straight to the top. My part was Inspector Craddock, an obsessive, single-minded detective determined to find the people who had got away with millions in gold bullion. As we tracked down each one over the thirteen weeks, we got nearer to Mr Big, who in the end shot himself.

'I remember it was all brought together very quickly with a great number of writers,' says Peter, 'but we had some first-class directors who are big names now. It was extremely demanding; we had to burn the midnight oil to do it. It was very rewarding though and turned out to be a milestone in my career.'

It was the turn of a female detective inspector to capture viewers in *The Gentle Touch* in 1980. This starred Jill Gascoine as Maggie Forbes, a widow whose policeman husband had been killed on duty. Television was saying,

'Yes, we know women work in all sorts of jobs too' – an attitude many women who increasingly had to support family life in a changing social climate might have thought overdue.

Jill Gascoine had spent many years in repertory theatre. Then she got a part in an LWT comedy followed by a big break in a play. 'I played a neurotic woman in her late thirties who in one scene takes an eighteen-year-old boy to bed. It sounds a bit daring, but in fact it was very tastefully done. It was because of that role that I started to get noticed and was given roles in other ITV series, including LWT's *Within These Walls* with Googie Withers.'

Jill had never played a policewoman before when she was cast as Maggie Forbes. 'The first programme was shown in 1980 on my birthday, 11 April, and that certainly felt like a good omen. That's the way it turned out because it got into the top ten ratings, reaching number four.' Jill Gascoine made fifty-six episodes of *The Gentle Touch* and remembers it with affection. 'It was a hard slog with a two-week turn round but it had a good team. We all got on well together on location and in the studio,' she says.

Did being a star of a police series affect her private life much? 'No, not really. It was nice being recognized. Obviously I was the butt of a few jokes like, ''OK, I'll come quietly, luv,'' but people are very nice in England and I didn't find anyone annoying at all.'

Popular series linger a long time in the public's mind and the characters are held in a particular kind of affection that lasts a surprisingly long time. 'Oh yes; just recently two taxi drivers have asked me when I'm coming back as Maggie,' says Jill. 'Some people probably think

that it is often the actors who don't want to do any more. Sometimes that's the case but it may be companies that decide they want to try something different.'

•

POIROT PROVES HIS CASE

The novels of Agatha Christie have proved a wonderful source of television crime stories. LWT first found it so in 1980 with an expensive three-hour adaptation of her *Why Didn't They Ask Evans?* John Gielgud, Eric Porter and Francesca Annis were among the large cast. The success of that led to a film from another Christie story, *The Secret Adversary*; Francesca Annis and James Warwick played her Tommy and Tuppence characters in it. Ten other

From a rich and pampered life in India a girl is sent to an English school but ends up living in poverty in Edwardian England. *A Little Princess* (1987) was a winner in the best story-telling tradition and starred Amelia Shankley, Maureen Lipman and Nigel Havers

★

LEFT

Mia Sara starred as Queenie in the 1988 mini series about a successful film actress who hides the fact that her mother is an Indian woman (played by Claire Bloom). LWT's involvement in this popular form paid off here and kept 10 million people up till midnight. Topol played the impresario who understood Queenie.

stories followed from that in a series called *Partners in Crime*.

Agatha Christie's famous detective, Hercule Poirot, appeared on the screen this year in the Poirot film series. The stories are not her most intricate, but Poirot himself is a meaty character. David Suchet's study of him has been the best yet and most in keeping with the character Agatha Christie actually created – clever and fastidious, not the comic continental some actors have made of him.

'I have the same eye for order as Poirot – I like things to be symmetrical. If I put two things on the mantelpiece they have to be exactly evenly spaced, that sort of thing. But I am nowhere near as fanatical as Poirot – I don't need exactly the same sized eggs for breakfast as he did!' comments David.

The perception and deductive reasoning of Hercule Poirot were not much in evidence in the 'slam-bang' series *Dempsey and Makepeace* in 1985, which starred Glynis Barber and Michael Brandon. The series was criticized by some for being too violent. The audience, however, turned up to watch the attractive, well-off Harry (Harriet) Makepeace team up with the rough diamond cop from New York, who was simply called Dempsey.

An even more popular dynamic duo called Doyle and Bodie had enjoyed a six-year run before them. *The Professionals* were a special armed criminal intelligence squad controlled from within the Home Office. Their job was to deal with those who did more than just break the law. The CI5 unit was the creation of Brian Clemens, a very successful ITV writer of action series. His formula of plenty of plot, not too much introspection, worked for

viewers – fifty-seven episodes were made and often repeated. Martin Shaw as Doyle, and Lewis Collins as Bodie, saw a lot of action between 1977 and 1983. Martin Shaw has good memories of the series. '*The Professionals* was of its time, and in its time it was the best. It was fun to make.'

Gordon Jackson, who played the squad's boss, Commander George Cowley, says of it, '*The Professionals* was great fun. But it was very different from *Upstairs, Downstairs*, which ended two years before. In that series the characters had to pay attention to what I was saying, but in *The Professionals* Bodie and Doyle would just ignore me. So, my motto was, when in doubt, shout!

'I can't say Commander Cowley was a subtle performance – just lovely tongue-in-cheek stuff. The shooting on film was similar to the shooting we used to do for films at Ealing Studios so I didn't find it too bad. But Martin Shaw and Lewis Collins had to work hard. They were in it all the time.'

AN ALL-TIME GREAT

The early years of LWT were marked by a smash hit – *Upstairs, Downstairs* (1970–75). The series was immensely popular with the public and critics alike and became a national institution. Viewers were hooked on an array of characters, notably one – an ultra-proper Scottish butler called Hudson, played by Gordon Jackson. The series also scored a remarkable success in America – unusual for a British programme.

Created by actresses Jean Marsh and Eileen Atkins, it was about masters and servants in a London house from 1900 to

Dempsey and Makepeace in 1985 was a good attempt to follow *The Professionals* and give the ITV network a popular action series. Glynis Barber was the upper-class 'Harry' Makepeace and American actor Michael Brandon her partner 'on loan' from New York where his abrasive style would not be missed by his boss

★

LEFT
Martin Shaw and Lewis Collins saw a lot of action as Doyle and Bodie in *The Professionals* which ran from 1977 to 1983 and was always popular on repeats. Its mix of plot and action appealed to viewers wanting escapism at the weekend

★

WHERE THE MONEY GOES

Why does drama cost so much? Because it takes so long to make and involves a lot of people and salaries – actors, production crew, designers, script editors, managers. The most expensive single ingredient is usually time, but actors, location filming and construction work can add up as well.

One five-minute film sequence can be done in a day provided that everything goes well. When the drama is a period piece, it can involve redesigning streets, taking down TV aerials and covering up yellow lines. Even contemporary scenes usually involve some design and construction work.

There are tricks of the trade that will save money – such as using 'glass shots'. In one Poirot episode, for example, viewers saw Istanbul. In fact the ship sitting in the harbour at Istanbul was nowhere near there. The scene was shot through glass painted with the mosques and minarets of Istanbul.

How can television save more money – to use on more drama? Not by using fewer extras or props. Speeding up the shooting is the way. If you can shoot in four weeks instead of five, a fifth of the cost has been trimmed off all areas of the budget.

1930. The concept was simple but clever. The lives of masters and servants could be dealt with separately and together. Another major reason for its success was the variety of characterization. The casting was skilful, and actors had the chance to go on developing their roles. The look of the period and the atmosphere in the household were conveyed with great style. Sixty-eight episodes were made and the careers of many actors blossomed as a result of it.

Jean Marsh and Eileen Atkins both had a parent who had been a servant. 'People never seemed to write intelligent parts for servants in plays,' says Jean Marsh, 'so Eileen and I thought that it would be a nice idea to do. We talked it out and did some outlines of plots and I spoke to an independent producer called John Whitney (who later became Director General of the IBA). He liked the idea very much and he took it to the Controller of Programmes at LWT, Stella Richman, and she bought the idea. I wrote the part of Rose specifically for myself because I am a real cockney.'

Says its producer, John Hawkesworth, 'We didn't think it would go beyond one series, but it turned out that *Upstairs, Downstairs* was the right idea at the right time. The public knows what the stuff of drama really is and that is why they liked it – good stories, good characters in situations where they are often under pressure. We were looking

at servants from their point of view and that hadn't been done before.'

When Gordon Jackson was approached about the role of Hudson it sounded like just another part. 'I don't think any of us thought it would grow into all those episodes and become such a big success,' he says. 'Mine was a jolly good part because it had a link with the upstairs and the downstairs, with all the cast.'

Someone suggested that he should listen to advice from a butler in Belgravia and watch him at work. He was given tips, such as that a butler would not eat with the rest of the staff and wouldn't change his jacket in front

of the staff, nor would a butler ever say 'follow me', because people always followed the butler anyway. 'But I left all these things to the producer and script editor. Our job was to provide good entertainment as a group of actors and that was the way to do it best,' says Gordon.

He had never played a servant before but he had played military types and the attitude in the role was similar. His most vivid memories are about learning the lines. 'I just tried to say them clearly with a certain authority. My main problem is that I am a slow learner of lines. If you watch how long it took Mr Hudson to read *The Times*, you'll see

FAR LEFT
**The *Upstairs,
Downstairs* people . Angela
Baddeley, Gordon Jackson and
Jean Marsh and in the back row
Christopher Beeny, Jenny
Tomasin, Jacqueline Tong,
Karen Dotrice and Gareth
Hunt**
★

ABOVE LEFT
**Gordon Jackson
built up his role of Hudson to be
the strongest but he remembers
Angela Baddeley (Mrs Bridges)
as 'a rock' of the series**
★

ABOVE
**Jean Marsh designed the part
of Rose the maid for herself**
★

DRESSING FOR THE PART

Actors and actresses never buy their own clothes for a part and they never wear their own. The costume department staff talk to the stars about their costumes and then decide where they are to come from. 'You have to pay close attention to what the writer, producer and director have in mind and dress the characters accordingly,' says department head May Tapley.

Over the years, LWT has built up a large store of costumes – a mixture of all kinds of clothes for drama and light entertainment, whether it is modern, period or drag. The costume department doesn't make clothes. Every show has a budget for costumes and, depending on what is available, they take costumes from the company's stock, or hire them, or have them made outside by specialists.

'Sometimes it's hard to say to major stars what they can or cannot have, but often they are not the hardest people to deal with,' says

May. 'Those playing smaller parts can be more difficult. Sometimes it is easier to dress people who are fastidious and it can be awkward to deal with someone who doesn't seem to care very much.'

Most of the costumes for a period drama are hired from one of the major London costumiers. 'There are hundreds of suppliers in London but, increasingly, as rents have risen, specialist costumiers of all kinds have moved outside.

'LWT doesn't keep any lists of measurements of actors, not only because people can change in size, but also because different roles may demand that they change. David Suchet's suits for Poirot, for example, were designed with him wearing padding so that he was made to look a little stooped to age him slightly and get the image of Poirot they wanted. The director wanted cool colours and crisp lines to convey Poirot's clipped and precise manner.

'For one character in *Wish Me Luck*, who had to wear the same dress for a long time, there had to be several dresses in various stages of wear and tear. For a war programme, clothes are hired from a specialist costumier and checked for authenticity when they arrive at the studio.'

Caring for the company wardrobe can be a bit fraught. Recently the LWT costume store had an unusual attack of moths and May had to get rid of many costumes,

particularly woolly things, early military costumes, furs and feathers. Then there was the time when one of Stanley Baxter's costumes literally fell off the back of a bike on its way to the studios. Radio London helped out with an SOS and somebody found it in the street and brought it to the studios in time.

The clothes go back to the hire company or into LWT's store after the production. That too can be a problem. 'For one comedy, an American football helmet and suit were bought. Later when someone went to get them out of stock again, the helmet had become a motorcycle helmet and the suit a space suit,' May laughs.

The people who make clothes for television are

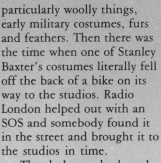

specialists and are paid accordingly. May's department has paid out cheques of £1,000 for a costume for some programmes. 'But for others it could be £2 at an Oxfam shop for a jacket or dress. Finding clothes for relatively modern productions can be just as much of a challenge as for a period one '

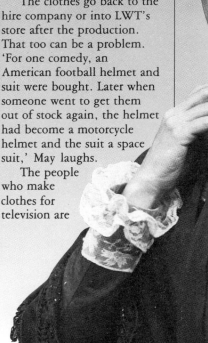

what I mean,' laughs Gordon.

'The series had a marvellous outcome for all of us because it provided a window on the world for us. We got other work from it. I got jobs in Australia, for example, on the strength of it – series like *A Town Like Alice*, which starred Bryan Brown. Then we went to the United States and went on the PBS Network who bought the series to help them raise money for their programmes. We went to Germany, Sweden and other countries – the series was very good to us all.

'Hudson was supposed to be getting older as the series moved on,' says Gordon. But he and Jean Marsh used to say that as everyone else in the series was getting older they stayed young. 'Young Simon Williams aged beautifully but I am very wary about wearing wigs and using stoops and things.'

Because Gordon takes some time to learn lines he becomes very single-minded and focused on what he is doing and can seem rather aloof. 'People think I am a very dedicated actor, but in fact it is sheer fear and wanting to get it just right. Because I know the TV camera reveals everything! Television is not like the cinema, where you get more opportunity to do something several times, if necessary, to get it right. The scenes you have to do on television are longer at a time anyway.

'I have never watched any episode of *Upstairs, Downstairs*. About twenty years ago I vowed never to watch myself again. I don't want to know my mistakes – that I twitch my little finger or whatever when I shouldn't and all the little things that the television camera picks up – I'm a bit too old for that,' Gordon says. 'But I think it is a good thing for young actors to watch themselves so that they can try to improve their performances.'

Angela Baddeley, he adds, was a real tower of strength in the series playing the part of Mrs Bridges, the cook. 'She also knew the real people upstairs and could tell "a lady" a mile off. If a rather affected young actress came on the set, she would say, "She's never a lady Mr 'udson." Although she was suffering badly from asthma she never complained, whereas the rest of us would have a bit of a grumble if we had a cold in the head.'

Upstairs, Downstairs had a host of meaty characters. Jean Marsh does not take too much credit for that however. 'Actors and writers create characters and the casting is very important. Gordon Jackson, for example, was brilliantly cast and making Nicola Pagett, who is very attractive, play such a hard character as Elizabeth Bellamy gave scenes an edge.'

Jean Marsh says that those years were a very happy time in her life because everyone got on so well together. 'The crews loved working on the series because they were proud of the work. They wanted to make a contribution whenever they could and would come and sit with you in the canteen and make suggestions about scenes and camerawork.'

The success of *Upstairs, Downstairs* in the United States was a breakthrough for British television. The Americans didn't buy it straight away. Says Jean Marsh, 'No one really thought it would be a success over there, our very English series. Then the Public Broadcasting Service network bought it and it was an instant hit. Major critics reviewed it and wanted to talk to me. We really thought we had made it when *Time* magazine featured the series.' Although she chose

LEFT
The costume department either has the clothes already, or has to hire or buy them. Francesca Annis had to have a large wardrobe for *Lillie* (1978), the serial about the actress Lillie Langtry, mistress of Edward VII and toast of New York. Prunella Scales and Geraldine McEwan are dressed 1920s style for *Mapp & Lucia* (1985) and Alfred Burke, Simon Cadell and John Malcolm in German uniform – carefully checked for authenticity – in *Enemy At The Door* (1978)
★

Millions remember
being gripped by *Bouquet of
Barbed Wire*, the story of
adultery and a father's
obsessive love for his daughter.
Frank Finlay played the father.
Thirteen years later he has
been acting in Australia but is
still recognized and asked
about the role. For Susan
Penhaligon it had an enormous
effect on her career. Frank, she
says, was great to work with
'and a bit of a giggler like me'

★

to cast herself as the cockney maid Rose,
Jean never found herself typecast or
called Rose by anybody. 'But I must
admit that when people recognize me in
restaurants and send over a bottle of
champagne – it's nice.'

John Alderton had a strong role as a
'baddie' in *Upstairs, Downstairs* after his
hit comedy series, *Please Sir*. 'I wasn't in
the first series at all,' says John. 'But the
producer came up with this idea of the
Welsh ''baddie'' chauffeur and, as
·Gordon Jackson always tells me, the
devil plays the best tunes! It was nice to
play a baddie for a change.

'I knew all the cast because Pauline
Collins, my wife, was in it,' says John

Alderton. 'But it was very strange, going
into a ready-made family. What was also
very odd was that it was always those of
us who played the servants who moved
the props back into position when the
director said ''Let's go back a bit.'' I
always remember that the ''masters''
seemed to get better dressing rooms than
we ''servants'' and doors opened for
them, whereas we were the ''working
class''.'

The series was ended at 1930, which
the producer, John Hawkesworth,
thought was a turning point. 'LWT of
course had a popular show on their
hands and were none too pleased about
it ending, but my company owned the
rights and there was nothing they could
do about it.'

But the series gave John another idea
that could have proved just as popular –
a comedy series with Hudson and Mrs
Bridges. When they got married he
wanted them to move to Hastings and
set up a guest house, where in the
summer they could have the children of
the aristocracy and their nannies
spending their holidays at the seaside.
The death of Angela Baddeley ruled that
out. 'I would have loved to do that,'
says Gordon Jackson.

●

THE POWER OF PASSION

IN 1976, a year after *Upstairs,
Downstairs* ended, viewers were
enthralled by a series which contrasted
markedly with the happenings of an
orderly Edwardian household where
passions were controlled, or at least
concealed. In *Bouquet of Barbed Wire*
the household was torn apart by uncon-
trolled passions.

CREATING A SCENE

London Weekend makes all its sets for film drama but for studio projects sets are made by various contractors around the country, arrive at LWT in sections and are assembled there.

'After that we "dress" them in the studio with things like furniture and curtains and props, which we either have, buy or hire,' says Mike Jarvis, construction manager. 'Sometimes we can only use a real house for certain things or at certain times. Then we have to try and match the same thing in the studio for shooting other scenes.'

How expensive is set-making? 'An average set would cost about £5,500,' says Mike. 'A dining-room, a kitchen and a living-room would be three sets. The more expensive-looking the room and furniture, obviously the more expensive the set; it could cost up to £25,000. For period drama you can have lots of panellings, dados and mouldings etc., whereas for modern settings they can look more bare.'

Hawk-eyed viewers often write in and complain that something is not authentic for the period. 'It is amazing the kind of thing that viewers pick you up on. They can spot doors, handles, clocks, radios, anything that is wrong for the period – often because they have the item themselves.

'One of the things we thought might make life a lot more difficult for us actually made it easier – that was going from black and white to colour. Trying to get colours that would give better definition and better shading in black and white was harder in those days than producing true colours on the screen now,' says Mike.

From the designer producing his drawings to getting the set made outside and in the studio takes about fifteen days. 'The sets may seem expensive, but not when you consider how quickly they have to be made and the effort that goes into them.'

Frank Finlay starred as the father whose affair at the office and obsessive love for his daughter, played by Susan Penhaligon, created havoc in the family. Susan had been in a lot of television plays before, but *Bouquet of Barbed Wire* was the production that really brought her to the public's notice.

Thirteen years later Frank is still very much associated with the role he played. He has been in Australia starring in a Jeffrey Archer play and he says, 'Even in Adelaide so many years later I am stopped in the street and recognized as Peter Mahon, the father in *Bouquet of Barbed Wire*.

'But I remember that it was only when we were part way through recordings of episode three that word began to get round that we were causing a bit of a stir among the limited number of media people who had seen private viewings.'

Frank is hoping that someone from LWT 'will one day wander into my dressing room with a novel for me to read that will be another quiet beginning to a wonderfully successful series.'

'It had an enormous effect on my career because it was the first time that my name really meant something to the television audience. I was surprised that *Bouquet* took off the way it did, because I thought the first episode was slow.' The public, however, had spotted the ingredients of riveting domestic drama.

'Mine was a very good part – I was self-centred and spoilt,' says Susan. 'I loved acting with Frank Finlay. He was fun and, like me, a bit of a giggler. His character was jealous of my *Bouquet* husband, and I think incest was implied but we never played it that way and we didn't talk about it. I had trouble finding my character to begin with and the director wasn't too pleased with me, I thought. But then I began to base some of the mannerisms on a friend of mine and it started to work.'

The production certainly had its moments. 'We were rehearsing and making it during a very hot summer and one day nearly all of us ended up working in shorts or swim-suits. We must have looked pretty silly rehearsing some of the scenes like that! I got very upset doing one scene: I was meant to

Helen – A Woman of Today was notable because it looked at the stress of a marriage and its break-up from a woman's point of view. Alison Fiske and Martin Shaw played the couple
★

Paul Nicholas, fresh from his comedy success in *Just Good Friends*, went into *Bust*. The 1987 drama series followed a too-smart businessman who takes one chance too many and is declared bankrupt. Belinda Lang as his wife was one of the women who found his charm offset his weakness for always going for a new deal

★

RIGHT
LWT and Nigel Havers took a chance with the drama series *The Charmer*, making the popular sitcom hero into a sly con-man and eventually a murderer. The risk paid off and the audience was hooked on the company's biggest drama success of recent years. Rosemary Leach and Bernard Hepton also headed a strong cast

★

be pregnant and James Aubrey, who was my husband in it, had to hit me. He was meant to be beating me and we had rehearsed what to do in a sort of choreographed way, but when it came to it we mistimed and I got hit.

'During the scene where I die in childbirth, people got cross with me because I couldn't keep a straight face. I had to heave and ventilate and I just felt funny simulating it. The director had sent me to Hammersmith Hospital to watch a lady in labour – but that wasn't much help. The lady they chose for me to watch hardly seemed to breathe or move at all, so in the end I had to just imagine it all.'

Seeing things from a woman's point of view has been a noticeable trend in television in the last twenty years. A pioneering series was *Helen – A Woman of Today* (1973), starring Alison Fiske and Martin Shaw. Five years before, George Cole had starred in *A Man of Our Times*, and the producer Richard Bates (son of the novelist H.E. Bates) had wanted to do a sequel called *A Woman of Our Times*.

Helen was a tale of disasters that befell a woman when her marriage broke up. Did Alison Fiske, who played the part of Helen, find that she became introspective and depressed herself? 'No, I just shrugged it off when I left the studios, I didn't take the part with me off stage. But it was a strenuous time for me because I became pregnant and then had a miscarriage. I was glad to get to bed and sleep at night.'

The thirteen-part serial was written by more than one writer and directed by several people. 'That wasn't a great help in getting the continuity right – the style of the thing seemed to vary,' says Alison. 'But the producer, who thought it all up, was dedicated to it and it wouldn't have been the same without him. The working relationship with the actors was great. Martin Shaw was a terrific actor to work with.'

What if she had to do it again? 'I would try to bring more humour to the part, to offset the gloomy side more. There's a lot I could put right now; mostly to do with economy of movement and expression. You don't have to do much on television – but it is difficult to learn to do little.'

Martin Shaw had been in situation comedies like LWT's series *Doctor in the House* and in many plays before he was cast as the young executive in *Helen – A Woman of Today*. 'It was a very interesting idea,' he says, 'and that kind of crisis in a relationship is as relevant today as it was then – you could make a fascinating series now.

'I watched it all, and I remember the whole thing as a very happy experience. Alison Fiske was marvellous, although she was having a bad time with her pregnancy. But happy experiences such as we enjoyed don't happen so much these days. There is now so much pressure on everyone in television drama because it is so expensive.'

The tradition of compelling contemporary drama which began with *Bouquet of Barbed Wire* continues today with series such as *Stolen* by Deborah Moggach, shot in the south of England and Pakistan.

•

CADS AND CHARMERS

A surprising runaway success for LWT in 1987 was *The Charmer*. Yet LWT had some qualms about how it would go

down. The problem was that this was
not the Nigel Havers of the light-hearted
'sitcom'. This was a black character –
indeed ultimately a murderer.

'I was slightly anxious about the part
initially,' Nigel says, 'because I thought
it might turn a lot of people off – particularly females. They were used to
seeing me in comedy, whereas this
character was not a particularly nice guy
– he was conning women all the time.'

Since sequences were shot in a
different order to the one in which
viewers eventually saw them, Nigel
sometimes wondered after days of
rehearsal just who he was meant to be in
bed with. 'It got quite confusing sometimes,' he says. 'I was very surprised at
how successful it turned out to be. In
fact taxi drivers would say their wives
were absolutely hooked on it, which also
amazed me.'

But casting Nigel Havers was the key
to success. His initial instinct was that it
was a good story. 'I got all the scripts in
the same afternoon and I thought I
would read the first one that evening.
But in fact I read the whole lot through
the night because the story was so compelling. That's what decided me, but I
also thought it was time I played a
baddie rather than a goodie.

'It was a sort of Jekyll and Hyde role
and I frightened myself sometimes when
I saw the playbacks. The series gathered
momentum as the audience could see
how he operated – they were the ''flies
on the wall'', whereas the people in the
story could only see the bright side of
him.'

When he thinks of *The Charmer*
now Nigel's first thought is,
'It was a very good experience in terms
of the people I worked with –
particularly two old friends, Rosemary

Leach and Bernard Hepton – and feeling very comfortable playing in that pre-war period.'

His next LWT role is very different again – he plays a Second World War pilot who is shot down and badly disfigured in the first ten minutes of the series, which then goes on to show how his life is radically changed.

That other popular charmer, Paul Nicholas, got the chance to do something different in *Bust* in 1988, after his big success in *Just Good Friends* and being associated with musicals. 'The BBC weren't offering me anything but more sitcoms, and this was a drama and a different part.' Paul Nicholas doesn't have a great interest in finance or investment himself. 'My one concern in that direction is to strive to be economically free, so that I will be able to say no to things I don't like. Many actors want the same.'

'I have a couple of friends like Neil Walsh and know other people like him;

nothing upsets them. Neil was a guy with problems but none that really worried him. He was like an actor, in a way, always changing jobs and looking for new ones. I found that the self-employed people, such as taxi drivers, liked *Bust* – they are like actors, we're all self-employed.

'The scripts were stronger in the second series, but I never thought it would be the kind of show that would grab a big audience because of the more specialist subject matter. And there was no excitement with action or danger in it,' says Paul Nicholas. He did have to drive a digger in one episode in the series but he did it 'slowly'. When it came to using the chain saw in another he felt that was a bit tricky.

'*Bust* was a marvellous shoot with a great crew. We worked all over London, and in Bournemouth and in the Cotswolds. It was one of the best times I've ever had because it was a happy team,' he says.

Paul watched all the episodes, and when he was nominated for a *TVTimes* award that pleased him as much as anything. 'Because, you know, that is the public voting for you, and being mentioned alongside actors like Ian Holm is gratifying.'

He is concerned about getting typecast. 'That is the terrible thing about television. People associate you with particular things when really you are an actor who could take on a variety of roles. The good thing about a drama series is that you don't have to do it in front of an audience. In situation comedy you have to go out and hope that they will find it funny, make them laugh.' Nevertheless, an LWT comedy series in which he plays a vet is what he is doing next.

Getting himself out of a tricky situation as usual is Neil Walsh in *Bust*. Paul Nicholas says he drove the JCB 'slowly'
★

FIERY TALES

Over the years many people have had
the idea of doing a series centred on a
fire brigade, but it took writer Jack
Rosenthal to come up with a script that
combined the drama of the job with
humour and human interest stories. He
got the idea for *London's Burning*
because he had become very friendly
with a fireman working at Archway
underground station who used to do odd
jobs for him.

Says Paul Knight, the producer,
'Over the years he had told Jack lots of
stories, and after the Broadwater Farm
riots, when P.C. Blakelock was killed and

firemen had come under attack, Jack
decided to write the original film. He
got the balance right in the script and
created such a varied group of
individuals – just as you might find in
the fire brigade – that it caught the
public's imagination. The director and I
cast a lot of new faces for the series, and
that also helped to give it a reality and
freshness that the public seemed to like.'

'Everyone from the Chief Officer of
Dockhead fire station down helped to
make the series and its characters as
authentic as possible,' says Paul Knight.
'We needed that because we are also
dealing with their private lives and had
to get a good idea of how the characters
could be developed.'

**Rupert Baker
helping a 'casualty' in *London's
Burning***

★

TOP
**Casting a lot of new
faces and sending the actors on
a fire brigade training course
added to the credibility of
London's Burning. Richard
Walsh, Katherine Rogers, Sean
Blowers and Gerard Horan
were members of Blue Watch**

★

Y ou have a great notion for a TV series but you don't work in television. Could it be made? With difficulty. You would have to start learning about how ideas are developed and how it could be shot and costed.

Since LWT started *London's Burning*, it has had six very aggrieved letters, some accompanied by a solicitor's letter, saying that the company had pinched someone's idea. But what's an idea? A fire brigade is a fire brigade. Only one TV professional proposed a fire brigade format but his proposal wasn't the same as *London's Burning* with Jack Rosenthal's characters.

People can get very angry when their ideas seem to appear on the screen. One man has harried LWT, claiming that *Bust* was his idea. Understandably, the public are not aware of much that goes on in the television business. They don't know, for example, that a dozen or more scripts and ideas arrive at LWT every day, many from people in ITV and the BBC – and now from independent producers as well. Despite television's voracious appetite, few of these offerings make it on to the screen. They just aren't good enough or practical enough.

Many of the stories in the series come out of true incidents from the files of the London Fire Brigade headquarters. The whole series is shot in south-east London. 'We have the use of the Dockhead fire station which is just next door. But since we obviously can't be in there all the time we have reproduced the interior in the studio.

'We can't show the full horror of what the fire brigade sometimes have to deal with, but we are not pulling any punches,' says Paul Knight. 'Even though we have real firemen standing by, there have been two occasions when fires have got out of control. So now we all have a massive respect for fire.'

All the actors are sent to a fire training school for two weeks before they join the series so that they look as though they know what they are doing. 'They have all enjoyed working on the series and have really got to understand the effect the job can have on firemen. For example, firemen have a very high divorce rate because of the hours they have to work sometimes.'

●

WHO CHOOSES THE STARS?

There is no hard and fast rule about casting actors for parts. Often the director makes the choice with the help of the casting department.

'Reading the script comes first,' says Diana Parry, LWT's Head of Casting.

YOU HAVE TO BE STREETWISE

When LWT go on a drama location and take over a street, the crew are usually surrounded by people keen to see the artists, count the cameras and observe all the technicalities of shooting. 'If we are unlucky in our choice of road and it is near a school, then at lunchtime we are mobbed by five hundred curious children,' says location manager Martin Bond.

To set up a film unit within a road, the crew has to have permission from everybody living there. 'If one person says that they don't want us, we have to move on. We have to buy our way into a road. If we are causing residents any inconvenience, we have to pay them some money.'

It takes just one person to be antagonistic towards the crew – like hanging out of a window with a radio blaring – and the crew have to stop work. But most people, Martin says, are keen to help

Anthony Hopkins and Lise Hilboldt in *A Married Man* – a tricky situation arose at the London location before filming could be continued

film crews who want to use their property, although they often don't appreciate how many people, how many vans and how much equipment are involved. 'If it is a small shoot and we will be there for a week, we will pay the property owner.'

Trouble can be just around the corner, nevertheless. 'On *A Married Man* with

Anthony Hopkins we had a situation where we were leaving Norfolk to return to two weeks' location filming in a London mews,' Martin remembers. 'But the day before we arrived, workmen had knocked down the mews house next door to the one we were filming in and they started rebuilding that day. It cost us a lot of money to control that situation.'

When LWT has to film abroad it employs a location manager from the area concerned. He is sent the script and looks for locations. 'Your local man is very important,' says Martin. 'But even then you have to be diplomatic, meet the mayor and his town council and probably have dinner with them. You must anticipate some tricky situations. For example, for *Wish Me Luck* we took over a village square and hung swastikas around the area, and we had a lot of extras in German uniform walking through the streets. Some of

the old chaps in the village spat at the extras. It was just a symbolic gesture, of course, because they knew we were filming for television.

'On location there is a certain loss of privacy for everyone and living in a hotel can be difficult and tiring,' says Martin. 'The shoot in Rhodes for Poirot was no holiday. We left the hotel at six in the morning and worked till 7.30 in the evening shooting. We had three days off in six weeks and didn't see much of Rhodes.'

Many actors on location now ask for caravans to sit in and learn their lines. 'So we hire the caravans and wardrobe vehicles for changing in, and dining buses for eating. On Poirot we had twenty-seven vehicles travelling with us like a circus because we had to take with us everything we were going to need. Otherwise, you need toilets and telephones, for example. Once you can find a toilet for the crew, you're all right.'

'Some directors have a lot of ideas of their own, some have no ideas at all and wait for the casting department to bring in people or give them suggestions. Some producers involve themselves a lot in the casting. Certainly a part isn't offered to anyone without the producer's consent and in some cases not without the consent of the Controller of Drama.'

Diana sets a lot of store by using imagination when casting. One example was the casting of Martin Shaw as the forty-year-old seducer/crooner in the period play *Cream In My Coffee* by

FAR LEFT
Jeremy Irons got his first big television break in the series, *Love For Lydia*, as one of the men in Lydia's life. Mel Martin starred as the *femme fatale* in the title role
★

LEFT
Peter Davison was 'resting', as actors say, working in a tax office in West London when Diana Parry picked him – because he had a good country face – to play in *Love For Lydia* (1977) from the H. E. Bates novel
★

When the crew of *Scoop* went to Morocco, they arranged for a day's shooting at a colourful local market. The day before they were to do it, the crew went to have a look. Panic! The proud governor of the little town at the edge of the Sahara Desert had decided that the old market wasn't good enough for television and had closed it down. In its place was a brand new concrete one.

**Michael Maloney
and Renée Soutendijk on
location in Morocco for *Scoop***

Dennis Potter when at the time Martin was playing a completely different role in *The Professionals*. Like many good actors, Martin Shaw could play a wide variety of roles and Diana knew his work well.

Casting comedy can be just as difficult as drama. 'You know the saying, "Any fool can play Hamlet but comedy is a serious business." We treat comedy as we would a drama – as we did with *A Fine Romance* with Judi Dench and Michael Williams – and set out to find the right people. I try to avoid using people who have been in six other situation comedies. If an actor says he hasn't done any situation comedy, I say that's fine.'

Diana doesn't believe the actors who say they don't want to do television. 'Television is where they make much more money than in the theatre – unless they are major attractions in the West End – and are seen by many millions of people.'

Casting often involves compromise. 'Having read the script you have to compromise on your choice of actors sometimes, because some are not available, or they don't like the part, or the director is not quite sure about your suggestions. When you don't get the person you know would be perfect, everyone else seems very much a second choice,' says Diana. 'Generally though, we have so many good actors in this country that casting directors are spoilt for choice. Because there are so many, even popular actors can be out of work for a long time – something the public forgets. There are also such things as lucky breaks.

'I remember in 1976 when we were casting *Love for Lydia*, the serial from the H.E. Bates novel. We were looking for someone to play the farmer's boy and we picked a face out of the casting directory because it looked like a good country face. It was Peter Davison. Peter at the time was "resting", as actors say, but earning some money in a tax office in West London. He never looked back and is, of course, now a big star.'

Another well-known name who got a good break in that serial was Jeremy Irons. 'It is a pity that the serial couldn't be repeated,' says Diana, 'because the viewers would be interested to see people who are now big stars.'

There are never many problems casting young actors for small parts because there are so many of them and they are keen to get a chance on television. But casting actors of forty upwards, says Diana, can be difficult. 'If actors of that age are still only doing small parts there may sadly be a very good reason for it.'

The latest development is computer-casting. Diana doesn't think much of it so far because it bypasses experience of actually knowing actors' work and using imagination when you do know their work. 'The people doing this think you can simply pick up a script, see a June Smith, blonde hair, five foot four, and then punch up all the actresses with similar details and you will have a good choice. Fine, but in practice when you have actually read the script and not just a list of parts, you can end up casting someone who looks completely different.'

There may, however, be a market for a system that records actors with certain skills. 'I remember for *Cream In My Coffee* I needed someone who could make a crêpe Suzette. I chose an actor and his agent told me he could do that. I learned later he had rushed out and learned how to make them that day.'

PART TWO

All the thrills of contest

'OUR FIRST CLANGER was with cricket. In 1969 we had bought the rights of the Gillette Cup Final which had been a mainstay of the BBC for years,' John Bromley, Controller of Sport, recalls with a shudder. 'We asked the Secretary of the MCC what time the last ten Gillette Cup Finals had finished. The average finish, he said, was about 6.20pm. So we scheduled the finish to be at 6.45, thinking that we had plenty of time to wrap it up with interviews and the awarding of the trophy. The next programme after it was to be David Frost live from the studio.

'At 6.40 we realized that the exciting match would never finish in time. I told David's producer that we just had to go on and he would have to delay

John Bromley, Controller of Sport, joined LWT at the beginning and has seen the advent of colour, negotiated many ITV sports contracts, and has lost count of the number of cricket clubs he belongs to
★

The Frost Programme. He said, no way. I asked if he could open up with the credits and go to David who could say, ''Good evening – and let's go straight back to Lords.'' David said he couldn't do that with Prime Ministers and Heads of State in the studio. So we came off the air and the viewers threw everything but the kitchen sink at us. We had only been on the air a few weeks. In the end we showed some recorded highlights.

'There was a massive row and the MCC said that LWT couldn't be trusted with a game of cricket and they would hand it back to the BBC. We had to go to law because we had a contract. Our Chairman at the time was Aidan Crawley and, guess what, the Chairman of the MCC at the time was Aidan Crawley. In the end the law courts as good as said, ''This is a joke,'' and we lost the case. The coverage went back to the BBC.'

The story just goes to show that sport is not like any other aspect of television and poses problems for any organization – especially one that has commercial breaks. It can't be packaged neatly unless it is recorded and edited – and then it loses some of its suspense and excitement because you either know the result or sense what is going to happen.

When the event is top class, live sport makes riveting television round the world – and you certainly don't need subtitles!

Cricket may have had a brief innings with LWT, but generally there has been a remarkable degree of continuity in John Bromley's department. John himself, Dickie Davies and veteran commentator Brian Moore have been there from Day One, 1968.

Some of the favourite strands of sports coverage are now being snapped after very long runs. Twenty-one years on, ITV is going for specific contracts for live events. Saturday afternoon's *World of Sport* ended in 1985, and wrestling, which had been popular for years, has been dropped. ITV snatched the athletics contract from the BBC and had to learn a new trade.

'The first athletics programme we did was the United Kingdom Championships from Antrim in Ulster in 1985,' says commentator Jim Rosenthal. 'We didn't realize the enormity of what we were taking on. It was a terrible, wet day. We thought that the hurdles would start at 2.30 and then we'd have the 200 metres at 2.40. Instead I had to talk through about fifteen minutes of people

HOW IT ALL BEGAN

John Bromley was executive producer of sport at ABC Television in 1967 when he and Jimmy Hill were asked to run sport at the new company, LWT. It had been agreed that LWT would take over *World of Sport* for the new ITV network.

'We had a blank piece of paper,' says John Bromley, 'and started to work out who we should have. Jimmy was impressed by a chap he heard on radio called Brian Moore, so we signed him up and we signed a chap at Anglia Television called Bob Gardam who was directing football. Then we brought in a lot of the lads from *World of Sport*

Jimmy Hill – from football player and manager to ITV executive

at ABC who had lost the ITV contract.

'Eamonn Andrews, the host of *World of Sport*, said that he was going to go with the other London company, Thames, because he wanted to do different programmes – *This Is Your Life* and the *Today* programme. So we decided to have Richard Davies, who used to be Eamonn's stand-in, to host it. He immediately became Dickie Davies.

'We had *World of Sport* on Saturday afternoon but we wanted to have a good football programme as well for a Sunday afternoon. So we started *The Big Match* and

had Brian Moore as a commentator and Jimmy as the expert.'

One of the first things that LWT had invested in was a slow-motion machine, the first ever. 'It cost £60,000, which was a fortune in those days,' says John Bromley. '*The Big Match* on Sunday was the first time the viewers saw the play analysed and were taken behind the scenes. Jimmy became television's first football expert.

'For the 1970 World Cup, the first World Cup in colour,' John reminds us, 'we enlisted ex-football professionals Malcolm Allison from Manchester City, Pat Crerand of Manchester United and Derek Dougan of Wolves, and also Bob McNab of Arsenal, who had been left out of the England team. The four of them were put together and it worked. Suddenly ITV and LWT had made a major impact with sports coverage.'

putting hurdles on the track and non-events like that. Nothing happened on schedule. There were long lags and it was a horrendous afternoon.' But he still likes live television, warts and all. 'It has a sharpness and immediacy. If you don't get that little tightness of the stomach, you know something's not right.'

At least Jim Rosenthal had many years' experience of radio and television reporting to fall back on. Some of today's best-known commentators and presenters were simply thrown in the deep end. Jimmy Hill was well known as a player and secretary of the Professional Players Association when he was recruited in August 1967. He left Coventry City, where he was manager, to become LWT's Head of Sport and a presenter. He was one of those who had frequently been interviewed but now he was taking on a very different role after a limited amount of experience with the BBC.

Do footballers take easily to the screen? 'Some take to it easily and have a facility with words; others don't,' Jimmy says. 'I quickly learned one thing – you don't get another chance on television if you make a mess the first time. It turned out well for me – certainly my spell at LWT was a very, very enjoyable five years of my life.'

Ian St John got his first television work with Granada in 1977. A year later ITV took him to the World Cup in Argentina as a co-commentator. 'On the flight home John Bromley asked me if I wanted to come and work for them,' says Ian, 'doing *On the Ball* because Brian Moore wanted a change. They wanted to keep the programme going but call it *Headlines*!'

Ian won't forget his début as a presenter. 'I was pitched in front of the camera with an autocue but with no experience of fronting a show. I wasn't terrified because I was ignorant and didn't know what was going on around me. It was only years later, when I learned something about all the other jobs that have to fall into place to get a live show out, that I realized what a tightrope I had been walking.'

He had been working for months without learning one trick – and discovered it 'only because Dickie Davies said to me one day, "Have you got a stand-by?" I went, "What do you mean – stand-by?" He explained that if any machine sticks or if there is any sort of problem, you can always say, "Well, here's some news in this morning," and read out a few team changes or other news. I thought that was a good idea and went to one of the editors and asked for a stand-by.'

As it happens, only weeks later a machine did stick; the item he had linked didn't appear on the screen. 'I said, "Sorry about that, some gremlins in the works," and went on to the next link. Nothing came up again. By this time I was panicking. That was my most terrifying time in television. I gave a wee bit of team news and heard the producer shouting in my earpiece to go back to the first item. Luckily it came up. If it hadn't, I was really out on a limb, totally inexperienced, with my only little bit of stand-by already used.

'I am glad I didn't know when I started what I know now. What I find very strange is that no one from television took me aside and said, "Look this is what you do." Nobody said a word. I am a football coach and if I get someone new, I coach them. But in television it seems no one coaches you; you go straight into it. That always sticks in my mind. You stand or fall on what you do, and if you don't do well, you are

out the door! I would be frightened to look at old tapes of myself now – but I must have done well enough for them to give me a chance to improve. I don't look on it as work; I look on it as just very enjoyable. I was never afraid of interviews or having cameras pointed at me.'

Being thrown in the deep end was Dickie Davies's experience as well when he went into television in the 60s. 'I don't know anyone in my game who had any training,' he says. He had been a purser with the Cunard Line on the *Queen Mary* and *Queen Elizabeth*. 'I had been in charge of entertainment on the *Queen Mary* and done a lot of microphone work. But when I got into television there was just a camera and I couldn't see the audience. I joined Southern Television on a Monday and was told that I would be reading the news on Thursday.

'I sat with John Benson, one of the great voice-over men who worked on Jonathan Ross's Channel 4 show. John was our star announcer and he guided me, explaining the importance of seconds. He said he would put me on on Wednesday night in vision for five seconds. All I had to say was "And now for the next thirty minutes, *The Arthur Haynes Show*." John told me, "Make sure you press your mike key, look at the camera, wait for the red light and go." I got made up and was all ready for my first television appearance, having rehearsed it all and talked so much about counting seconds. I came up and I said, "And now for the next thirty seconds, *The Arthur Haynes Show*." I didn't realize what I'd said, but John said quietly, "It's going to be a little longer than that." That was it; you had no training apart from talking to people

A familiar face on Saturday afternoons – Dickie Davies presenting ITV's *World of Sport*. He remembers how he started – by being thrown in the deep end
★

who had done it themselves.'

He almost fell for a trick when he went to audition as a stand-in for Eamonn Andrews on *World of Sport*. 'Three people were down for auditions. I was the first one in and I had to do a mini *World of Sport*. I had my earpiece in to listen to the director and had to react to immediate situations.

'They sent in a piece of news and I read it. Then three minutes later they sent in the same piece of news, maybe by mistake. I said to the imaginary viewers, ''I'll update that piece of news later on,'' and I put it aside without reading it. They thought that was a great wheeze and they did the same again with the other hopefuls to see how they would react. The others read it again. I got the job.'

Brian Moore was signed from BBC radio and in twenty-one years has seen all the footballing greats and many World Cup finals from the commentators' box

★

GREAVSIE ON THE BALL

Someone who took to television like a duck to water is Jimmy Greaves. It came to him just as easily as football did. But Jimmy says that although he had been a commentator before, he didn't really want to do the 'Saint & Greavsie show'. 'It wasn't Saint and Greavsie in those days. It was *On the Ball*, part of *World of Sport*. Apart from working on a programme in the Midlands called *Star Soccer*, I was doing *The Saturday Show*, a children's programme. I enjoyed working with the kids and it was such a good programme that I really wanted to stay with it. I was also offered a job on another show and so I wanted to develop my career that way. But I think the television people must have got together

and decided that it would be better if I did a network football show with Ian St John. 'I enjoy doing the show, it's fun. Ian and I get on well together and we have developed it over the years. By and large we are left alone. We go in on a Saturday when there are not many people about.'

Ian St John has now been the co-commentator – 'the colour man' – at the Cup Final, at the World Cup Final in Spain and on international matches. 'Presenting the studio end of the World Cup Final in Mexico was the biggest thing I've done. The more you do, the more you become accustomed to it. I can listen to Jimmy, listen to the director's instructions and keep the show moving – it's become second nature. Most sports-people get their first taste of television being interviewed – which is easy. You sit there and someone asks you questions, no problem. But it's different to go in and present the programme and ask the questions yourself.'

Jimmy Greaves thinks, 'We have mastered the art of television to a degree. Ours is a live programme and you have to have the technical ability to operate in that situation. You've got to wear ear-pieces and be able to cope with what everyone else in the studio has to do. Ian has mastered the autocue. I can't because I'm a bit dyslexic. But I can make a one-line note on something and talk about it for ten minutes – which is unfortunate for everyone else.'

Football has been very good to Saint & Greavsie and they try to make the game seem fun and an outing to be enjoyed. However Jimmy says, 'Ian and I take football's image seriously. Some are cynical about it. Last March gave a prime example when a referee was wired up to cover a football game. How can the

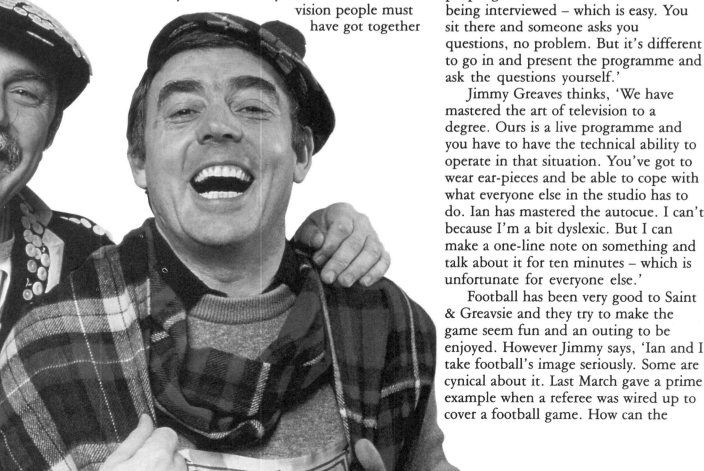

Ian St John and Jimmy Greaves, two ex-pros whose cheerful approach as Saint & Greavsie is intended to show that football should be a fun game for players and spectators alike
★

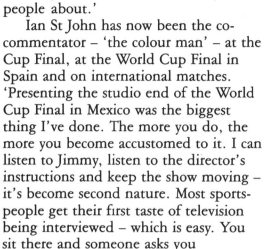

Football League have allowed it? You had to be pretty simple not to see what was going to happen. The things his mike picked up were not good for football and not good for television. Just sensationalism – that's all it was.'

THE QUESTION MARKS AGAINST ATHLETICS

Soccer has certainly had its fair share of bad publicity, but athletics now risks being totally discredited because of drugs. The Ben Johnson episode at the 1988 Olympics was a catastrophe because the performance of many outstanding athletes will from now on have a question mark against it. As Dickie Davies puts it, 'You don't know now whose performances are being enhanced. We will never know who was on drugs and who was cheating – because that's what it is.'

It is one story Jim Rosenthal wishes he had never heard – but it was one of his major scoops. 'We did the Carl Lewis story in the World Championships in Rome in 1987 when he was the first world-class athlete to speak out against athletes taking drugs. He told us about gold medals being won by drug-takers who were years ahead of the doctors and drug testers. That was my biggest and most unexpected news story.'

'Sadly there are not many sports that attract a good size audience,' Jim Rosenthal thinks. He doesn't believe that there is another sport waiting to be discovered by television in the way that snooker was. 'If we had great champions in, say, tennis, maybe people would want far more tennis coverage. But that doesn't apply in every sport. We could

have the world's greatest small bore shooter but no one is going to watch that on television.'

But the public's attitude to sport has been changing considerably in twenty-one years. They now have extensive experience of watching it on television in colour from around the world. They see the world's best athletes every four years in the Olympic Games and the world's best footballers every four years in the World Cup. National events and league soccer can seem ordinary in comparison. Saturday afternoons, too, are different – shops are open now and home ownership has led to DIY on a huge scale. Sixty per cent of homes have video recorders and people can programme their own entertainment.

Saturday's *World of Sport* came off ITV in 1985 after a twenty-year run. The feeling in the ITV network was that ITV should be more flexible at the weekend and go for exclusive sports events. In any case a lot of Saturday sport was recorded tape, and the viewers were losing interest

The ITV football panel. In the studio for the World Cup in 1970 here with Brian Moore were (left to right) Malcolm Allison, Derek Dougan, Jimmy Hill, Pat Crerand and Bob McNab. Television had recruited top players and managers who really knew the game and the coverage was a big success
★

LWT and its *World of Sport* have known justifiable satisfaction over some outstanding coverage of major world events – but there has also been disappointment. A high spot was the well-planned and lively presentation of the 1974 World Cup, held in Munich, when the controversial football manager Brian Clough joined the ITV team of experts. This happy exper-

ience was soon followed by dejection – first at the ITV network's decision not to cover the 1976 Olympic Games in Montreal. Then, two years later, LWT were to cover the World Cup in Argentina but because of a union row they had to send a film unit instead of much faster electronic cameras – which the BBC had. Being behind the BBC with the

stories all the time was galling.

The next Olympics, 1980 in Moscow, saw LWT with its most ambitious coverage and this time it worked well, to the delight of the ITV network and the great enjoyment of viewers. The 1982 World Cup in Spain was also a hit and saw the new partnership of Saint & Greavsie. Such good times were to be

marred again. A great deal of work had gone into covering the 1984 Olympics in Los Angeles. But again there was union trouble, Controller of Sport, John Bromley, sums it up: 'We effectively put £2 million in the ash can.'

Successful coverage of the World Cup in 1986, and the Olympic Games in Seoul in 1988 restored the buoyancy of the department.

UNWELCOME ROLE

Tragedies that take over the international headlines have happened before the eyes of commentators and surprised them with a role nobody could ever be ready for.

Such a time came for Ian St John when he was doing local radio coverage of the Liverpool v. Juventus European Cup Final at the Heysel Stadium in Brussels in 1985. 'That was the worst event anyone could have to witness. It will live with me for ever.' Trouble between opposing supporters boiled over and forty-one Italian and Belgian fans died in the riot.

The game is still suffering from that evening – which came only two weeks after the horror of the Bradford City fire where forty fans died.

For Dickie Davies, it is terrorism at the Munich Olympic Games of 1972 that is seared in his memory. A group of Black September Arab guerrillas broke into the Israeli camp with machine guns. Israelis were killed, one weightlifter died after holding a door while his friends escaped and ten other athletes were taken hostage. One, a runner, ran for it with Arabs firing after him and escaped.

Twelve thousand police surrounded the village and the Games were suspended.

'I spent virtually a whole day on top of a ladder with binoculars and walkie-talkie,' says Dickie, 'telling viewers what was going on.' When the guerrillas were on their way to a plane waiting at the airport, the German police turned on all the airport lights and opened fire. The nine Israeli hostages were killed.

'It was about six in the morning when news came of what had happened. I went round the village to find out

what the athletes felt should happen. Should the Games continue? Most said no. But some said they had worked for four years for it and wanted their chance to win a gold medal. While the Arab guerrillas had been holding the hostages in the Israeli camp, a swimming pool just over the fence was full of people splashing about having a good time. You would have thought it was a holiday lido.'

The Olympics resumed the next day after the tragedy. 'I always remember the first final after that,' says Dickie. 'It was the women's 100 metres hurdles and the Israeli athlete should have been in the line-up but there was an empty lane. That told the story for me.'

in that unless it was very recent and exciting. They wanted live action.

Dickie Davies was naturally sorry to see the programme go. 'We knew it was going to happen. The network wanted racing, whose audience was diminishing, to go on Channel 4. They wanted live sport on a Saturday afternoon, and didn't think we should compete with the same type of programme as the BBC any more. They also wanted a change of image on the network. For example, wrestling had a down-market image, but now LWT's biggest single advertisers are the big financial institutions who want to aim up-market. So we bought the athletics contract and tried to buy the rugby union contract. We have had all the major fights from America over the years and wanted to keep doing those.'

The next stage was to get live football. It came in September 1985 when ITV presented League Football live for the first time. 'Tottenham v. Nottingham Forest was our first live

match on television,' Dickie remembers well. The new set-up had made some changes in his working pattern. 'The *World of Sport* team used to begin their week on a Tuesday with their 'homework': talking to people in sport, reading the league tables, going to press conferences, and looking at what they would be covering that week. 'We would have a meeting on Thursday to tie it all up,' says Dickie Davies, 'and on Friday I would start writing scripts, doing promotions and pre-programme recordings that might need voice-overs. I would come in about eight on a Saturday morning, have a good breakfast, meet the kids and talk about what we were going to do. We didn't rehearse very much, just for the opening and *On the Ball* because it was a tight little show. After that I would spend about fifteen minutes in make-up, which is quite a nice quietening down spell, just like going to the barber.'

But there was one time the soothing

routine didn't work. 'I remember there were ten minutes before going on air and the fire bell sounded. It was a bomb scare. We were ushered out very quickly into the street. The editor was talking to ITN from the phone across the road trying to tell them to keep the news on air till we got back in again. It turned out that the current affairs people had been doing a story about terrorism and used a facsimile of a bomb. When someone was moving furniture on their floor that weekend they found this bomb and thought it was real. We rushed back as quickly as we could.'

●

FAVOURITES AMONG THE SPORTS ACES

The spirit of sport that existed in 1968 has disappeared. Violence, tragedy and greed have tarnished the image of many sports. Sportsmanship has been replaced by cunningly staged tantrums on the tennis court, the 'professional' foul in football which can ruin a player's career, and trading punches on the rugby field.

Our children should be brought up to believe that great sports people do not behave like that. We have at least one, who has not reached the very highest rung, except in popularity. He sets a good example and the British public have taken to him. Frank Bruno is without doubt the country's most popular sportsman. Why? 'There are certain people the British public take to and Frank is one of them,' says Jim Rosenthal. 'It couldn't happen in any other country that when someone gets beaten they come back to the kind of welcome Frank got this year after the Mike Tyson fight. You hear lots of stories about top sports people misbe-

having, not turning up, drugs, drink, etc. I have never heard of one about Frank Bruno. He is very reliable – which is important in our business – and he has a great natural image which I don't think is feigned or has had PR people working on it.

'He was up at Gateshead playing football in a celebrity game. He also took part in a celebrity run and was like the Pied Piper with a couple of thousand kids running after him. Kids like him, and you could say that's the reason the public like him. He is from a game you might not think would produce a nice gentle guy, but he is naturally one of "the nice men".'

Another fighter, Mohammed Ali, really was one of the greats who joked his way into the public's affections. He was a big draw for *World of Sport*. 'I went over to do an interview with him at Caesar's Palace in Las Vegas,' says Dickie Davies. 'I went to meet him with Reg Gutteridge at ten in the morning in the coffee shop. When Reg introduced me he walked straight past the both of us. At eleven we were ready with the camera and he came and looked down at me – I looked up at him. He started shadow boxing and his fist was landing half an inch from my chin – he was having fun testing me out. But I began to see the face creasing into a smile and he put his arm round me and we talked.

'When he came over here we did a studio programme with sports and show business personalities. After I did the interview we threw it open to the audience to ask questions. The Queens Park Rangers footballer Terry Mancini stood up and said, "Mohammed, I'm a professional footballer and I would like to ask you a question." Mohammed looked at him. "You can't be a profes-

One of boxing's true greats – Mohammed Ali of the dancing feet and quick wit. An interview with him could make very entertaining, but often unpredictable, television

★

LEFT
Big Frank – probably the most popular sportsman in the country. 'You hear lots of "stories" about top sports people misbehaving,' says Jim Rosenthal, 'but I have never heard one about Frank Bruno'

★

Until she retired from the scene, controversial Zola Budd was one of the runners best loved by the British public
★

sional footballer, you're bald.'' Terry quick as a flash came back at him and said, ''The guy who put you on the deck didn't have much hair either Mohammed.'' That was Henry Cooper he was talking about.'

Who are the easiest sports people to interview? 'Anybody who wants to talk to you,' says Jim Rosenthal ruefully. 'Boxing and boxers give you most co-operation and general friendliness. They are always very amenable even straight after fights. Maybe that's to do with the kind of person who goes into fighting. He depends very much on himself, his strengths and weaknesses are there to see – there's nowhere to hide. That kind of person isn't afraid or unhappy to chat. Anyway, in the ring, field or track I have had a lifetime of losers crying on my shoulder – I have the loser's interview off to a fine art.'

One of the hardest people to

interview has been the South African runner Zola Budd. 'One of the reasons,' says Jim Rosenthal, 'is that English is not her first language – Afrikaans is. She was very reticent, shy and a bit suspicious and it was like pulling teeth but she got better. I used to think ''That won't sound very good,'' but the public seemed to warm to her. She was also popular with British runners. Zola had come from a protected background in South Africa and was all of a sudden thrust into the political spotlight that even a very experienced sportsperson would have found hard to handle.'

Jim Rosenthal found that world 400 metres record holder Butch Reynolds was impossible to interview at the 1988 Olympic Games in Korea. 'When I went to talk to him he ran away. There wasn't much point in running after a sprint champion.'

PART THREE

Bringing the best before your eyes and ears

'ARTS PROGRAMMES REFLECT what can be the great interest in many people's lives – the cinema, theatre, photography, books, music or whatever.' Melvyn Bragg, editor and presenter of *The South Bank Show*, believes that television at its best should reflect as far as possible the variety of interests of the public. 'Art' can mean Paul McCartney or Gustav Mahler, Laurence Olivier or Lenny Henry, John Le Carré or Marcel Proust, David Hockney or Toulouse-Lautrec. LWT's overall aim with its coverage is to be serious but also entertaining; to deal with a subject rigorously but at the same time make it accessible to a wide audience, scorning any élitist view that arts appreciation belongs to

one section of society. Having said that, LWT accepts that there will always be people who turn off these programmes – just as there are people who immediately turn off sports programmes. Programmes that make viewers think, that sound even a bit heavy, might not seem an appealing diet for a leisure-bent, work's-over-now, weekend audience. But getting an arts programme on the ITV network every week and keeping it there has been one of LWT's most important achievements. Two people have dominated that effort – Humphrey Burton, who started it in 1968 and was responsible for *Aquarius* from then until 1975, and Melvyn Bragg, who has edited and presented *The South Bank Show* for LWT since 1978.

•

THE SOUTH BANK SHOW

When Melvyn Bragg was hired by Michael Grade, LWT's Director of Programmes, he saw how the competition for the eyes and ears of the public had been changing. Daily and Sunday papers were getting fatter; colour supplements were blooming. Magazines of all kinds were also dealing far more with a wide

variety of visual and performing arts. There was increasing talk of a fourth channel and how different it should be from the mass-appeal channels. Melvyn set out his stall to compete with them all – and also knew that he could reach the parts they could not, because unlike newspapers and magazines, his programme went into every home free.

He believes an arts programme should be accessible to people and engage their attention but not by taking any easy way out. 'One of the things that interested me recently was a ratings comparison of *The South Bank Show* and BBC and Channel 4 arts programmes. We are much more "highbrow" than them, and yet our audience is way above theirs – four times as big in some cases.' An average audience is about 2 million and, in a *South Bank Show* season, 12 million different viewers will dip into the show over three months.

'We take on difficult subjects and try to do each one well when we have worked out what to do.' Working out what to do is something he sets a lot of store by. 'One of the first things I did at LWT was to strengthen the research. It is a crucial ingredient in our success but is very cheap in television-cost terms.

Film director David Lean, whose 1962 film *Lawrence of Arabia* has just been 'remade' incorporating previously unused footage, discussing his work on *The South Bank Show*

★

LEFT
The scope of arts programmes has widened considerably since the 1960s. In particular there is less emphasis on the 'great dead' and far more on all forms of modern arts which people now enjoy. *The South Bank Show* tries to embrace it all. Television subjects, such as writer Dennis Potter, comedian Lenny Henry, cinema star Robert Redford and musician Paul McCartney, are now familiar in arts programmes alongside classical music and literature

★

Shooting first and asking questions afterwards is uneconomic and very rarely works. When you have researched a programme well you can go and make it faster. So we ask a lot of questions, read, write scripts, talk it out and then go to it.'

Incidentally, when *The South Bank Show* advertises a job for a researcher it gets five thousand applicants, which is a yardstick of the attraction the programme has for young people.

What decides the films to be made?

'Researchers constantly bring me ideas,' says Melvyn, 'and ideas also come from film makers, writers, people who just write in – from a huge variety of sources. I have my own ideas and, when I think they are good, I tend to follow up quite a few of them.'

Arts programmes in the 1960s and 1970s tended to be reverential and to deal significantly with the 'great dead'. *The South Bank Show* sought to change that and to look at what was actually going on

The late Russell Harty managed to make a great film for *Aquarius* with surrealist painter Salvador Dali whose unusual and volatile talent could be a producer's nightmare
★

MEETING OF ECCENTRICS

The most eccentric talent the *Aquarius* programme had to deal with was the painter Salvador Dali who died earlier this year. The late Russell Harty – then in his first television job as an associate producer on *Aquarius* – interviewed Dali and narrated the programme. Called *Hello Dali* (1972), 'It was an absolutely superb piece of comic, manic reportage,' says Humphrey Burton. 'It caught Dali's surrealist spirit – and that without doubt could be a programme-maker's nightmare because of the unpredictability. In the end it turned out very well and the credit for that was definitely Russell's.'

now. It was the first arts series to devote programmes to television writers, and has since made films about modern music, comedy and writings of all kinds. Paul McCartney, Eric Clapton, Lenny Henry, Ben Elton, Raymond Chandler and Patrick Leigh Fermor jostle with artists from all over the world. There aren't any no-go areas.

'We get a lot of phone calls asking for information and letters from people who have enjoyed the programme. There is a barrage of input telling us that viewers want us to be there and cater for their individual tastes. There are conflicts, of course. For example, some people who like opera will watch anything you do about opera – but they loathe ballet and won't watch any of that. There is a growing interest in dance, though, that has surprised all of us on the programme. There are also oddities. Although we are a theatrical nation, no matter how good our theatre programmes are we don't do very well with them in the ratings. Maybe theatre lovers are simply not television viewers.'

It's not just the audience who have quirky characteristics. *The South Bank Show* subjects have them *par excellence*. The Swedish film director Ingmar Bergman, one of the cinema's greatest talents, made Melvyn Bragg pass an exam before he agreed to be a *South Bank Show* subject. 'I met him in Munich and had lunch with him and his wife,' Melvyn recalls. 'He has always had trouble with his stomach and I remember he was eating some awful-looking mixture that looked like semolina. He wanted to find out just how well I knew his work. Since he was and is my favourite film director, I must have done quite well and he agreed to do the interview.'

Some very talented people have a way

of taking over the show. When making *Laurence Olivier – A Life*, Melvyn found his subject overwhelmingly helpful. 'As a storyteller, his timing is unsurpassable. He is amusing and a brilliant mimic. By the time I came to do the programme he had worked out the story of his life as he wanted to give it to the world. He had written it, rehearsed it and he used me as the first person to see the performance.'

Some situations can be more awkward. Harold Pinter, the playwright whose enigmatic style is highly distinctive, was unpredictable and hard work. 'He wanted the programme to be good and I certainly didn't mind that. But the problem was he was unsure how to go about what he was meant to be doing; unsure even what he wanted to say or not say. He would want to get on quickly and then become very hesitant and turn prickly. It all began to look and sound like one of his plays. It was really all because he wanted to do something exceptional.'

An era of television arts is threatened now. The government's plans for ITV and television in general are seen by many as threatening not only the quality but the

Melvyn Bragg, editor and presenter of *The South Bank Show*, at the seaside during the making of a programme with playwright John Osborne and Laurence Olivier
★

range of programmes offered to the public. Yet no other ITV programmes have earned such national and international recognition in terms of awards as their arts programmes. The programmes' existence and the plaudits they have won have given ITV and the IBA a world-wide reputation and high status. Will the new broadcasting system support 'minority' programmes – in television terms, programmes that attract under 5 million viewers? All arts programmes, documentaries, nature programmes, current affairs, plays, and most of Channel 4's and BBC2's output are minority programmes. We shall have to wait and see along with Melvyn Bragg whether 'an act of faith will create the support and financial structure to maintain such a range of the public interests.'

•

A FLAIR FOR SHARING HIS ENTHUSIASM

'Pure enjoyment' is pioneering arts producer Humphrey Burton's description of working on a programme called *The Great Gondola Race*. It was about the race to save Venice and the annual race around the Grand Canal by the Venetian gondoliers. Venice, by the way, is Humphrey's favourite city in the world. 'It was working on several levels at once' – travelogue, drama, history, suspense, a chase – 'and we were using all the film resources of LWT with three cameramen deployed on the Grand Canal – what a wonderful day! The programme was spectacular to look at, but it was also thoughtful because it helped people to understand what had to be done to save Venice,' says Humphrey.

The Great Gondola Race was an edition of *Aquarius*, created and edited by Humphrey Burton whose commitment and enthusiasm to communicate could pull in 3 million viewers.

Humphrey Burton travelled further afield than Venice whilst engaged on *Aquarius* from 1968–1975 – indeed all over the world – for his programmes but his most memorable trip was to Iran in 1974 to celebrate the 2500 years of the Persian empire. 'That was the most spectacular, and the most demanding because I had to learn the names of all the Persian dynasties in about twenty-four hours. We were doing a portrait of Persia and the arts in Persia with a commentary by the Shah's wife Farah Diba, and I was to set the scene by describing the highlights of the past twenty-five centuries of Persian history.'

Often it was managing the subjects themselves, the people, rather than mastering the subject matter, that made Humphrey's work taxing. One difficult person he had to deal with on the screen was the American novelist Mary McCarthy. 'Although she appeared to be smiling at you, it was the smile of a piranha. You knew she was extremely well educated and didn't suffer fools gladly – or people who hadn't read her books as carefully as she had written them. I was very scared of her and I enlisted the help of the late Russell Harty to join me in the studio talking to her. We both made absolute idiots of ourselves in front of her and the viewers.'

Interviewing and filming conductor and composer Leonard Bernstein (composer of *West Side Story*) was another tricky job. 'You had to be prepared to analyse his work with him, and he was another American who would not be fobbed off with easy questions or answers,' says Humphrey. But even such

Humphrey Burton,
who was responsible for starting LWT's arts programming in 1968, dealt with some difficult characters and tricky situations but remembers those seven years with the company as the best of his life

★

programme-making had its cheerful side.

'We did the Verdi *Requiem* in St Paul's Cathedral with Leonard Bernstein conducting, and we had only one day of rehearsal for this enormous piece. That was when I was most terrified. And I had to go and explain my project to actor Gregory Peck of all people, who was somehow one of the producers we were dealing with. Oliver Smith, who designed *West Side Story*, was the designer and he became my mate. I remember we had a television studio floor plan on which St Paul's had been drawn, and in the top corner were the words "Designer: producer: scale." So Oliver wrote: "Verdi's *Requiem*: designer – Sir Christopher Wren: scale – enormous".'

Looking back on his LWT days, Humphrey Burton has no regrets – far from it. 'Without question it was the most important time in my working life. I was independent and became a figure in the public's mind because I presented so many editions of *Aquarius*. To be editing your own programme as well is to have real power.

'My early days with Huw Wheldon and *Monitor* and my time at LWT were the happiest days of my professional life.' The pioneering BBC arts programme *Monitor* was Humphrey Burton's training ground for *Aquarius*. He – and Melvyn Bragg – started working on *Monitor* with the late Sir Huw Wheldon. Sir Huw, a great enthusiast and communicator – and, incidentally, a legendary story-teller in television – wanted to talk to the public at large and not just to the converted. His two 'pupils' harbour the same wish.

Having been producer, director and editor of *Monitor*, Humphrey Burton saw that arts programmes had become much more diverse and thought there was a gap for a popular arts magazine that would not take itself too seriously. His chance came in 1967 when a colleague at the BBC, Michael Peacock, was leaving to help set up LWT. He asked Humphrey to join him.

Humphrey set out to appeal to ITV's kind of audience. Trying to entice viewers to new experiences was and still is part of the plan. So LWT started arts programming late on a Saturday night with a programme that was to encompass everything from popular entertainment to serious music, from a cabaret singer to the New York Philharmonic. The *Saturday Special*, as it was called, ran for two years. Its audience figures soon showed that its slot was wrong. People wanted entertainment on Saturday evenings. Following a popular comedy with arts – no matter how much mass-appeal the night's subject had – brought the big turn-off.

Something different was required, and in January 1970 the new arts magazine called *Aquarius* was born, with Humphrey as presenter and producer. It was to be a middle market programme on a Friday evening. 'Spruce yourself up, get your hair cut, buy yourself some decent suits and get on with it,' was the brief command of Cyril Bennett, Controller of Programmes.

The first *Aquarius* consisted of a ten-minute film by a very talented film-maker called Charlie Squires about pantomime animals; a piece by comedian John Wells; an item about an artist who covered the cliffs in Australia with plastic; and a debate about why *Aquarius* was not able to show a full frontal nude woman walking down a staircase – which was part of a film on

Sir Peter Hall took over presenting *Aquarius* when Humphrey Burton left to return to the BBC in 1975
★

Marianne Faithful (left) and Britt Ekland in a Strindberg play for *Aquarius*. Marianne – known as a pop star – turned in a fine performance and surprised everyone
★

the work of French film director Jean-Luc Godard.

Aquarius ran fortnightly on Fridays after *News at Ten* for one season. Then the other ITV companies argued for taking it off because its ratings weren't high enough. They lost because the IBA strongly supported keeping it going. Later *Aquarius* was shown on Saturdays, and later still it moved to Sundays at 5.30, where it got its biggest audiences.

People whose work had huge popular appeal were not always popular with Humphrey. Film directors, especially, seemed surprisingly unco-operative. 'The hardest I got was Alfred Hitchcock. It was not difficult to get just a word or two around the fringes of the set, but to get him to sit down and talk about film-making was a different matter. However, he couldn't match the rudest film director I encountered in those days – director of *Exodus* and *Advise and Consent*, Otto Preminger.'

A surprise of a different kind was Marianne Faithfull. 'I was doing a

feature on a play by Strindberg where there is one girl who talks a lot (she was played by Britt Ekland) and another who never says a word, played by Marianne. She amazed us all by showing how bloody good she was.'

David Niven provided some laughter on *Aquarius*. 'I literally fell about with David, he was great. He had recorded a trailer for us saying, "I want you all to know that my good friend Humphrey Burton will be with me in *Aquarius* this week." About a week later I was at the Old Vic and he walked straight past me without a hint of recognition – our "friendship" was rather short-lived.'

Humphrey Burton left LWT in 1975 to go back to the BBC. 'I had a big row with the ITV network because a Tchaikovsky symphony was too long by four minutes and it couldn't be fitted in. I can understand their view more easily now but at the time it was the straw that broke the camel's back.'

What did he do for LWT? He gave them prestige. 'I had the arts moved up into the first division. They hadn't been taken seriously before except in single short bursts. But having arts programmes on every week was something that singled LWT out.'

Why was it so important for ITV to have an arts programme? 'An appreciation of art is not restricted to the educated,' says Humphrey. 'Many forms of artistic expression are appreciated by people who left school at fourteen, particularly among the older members of the audience. On the other hand, there are plenty of yuppies you wouldn't find watching any kind of artistic work. Television goes into everyone's home and is a wonderful way of cutting through the so-called barriers of class, taste and money.'

PART FOUR

Angles on the real world

IT DIDN'T LOOK promising at all to start with but *The 6 O'Clock Show* with Michael Aspel and Danny Baker became a big success and ran for six and a half years. The idea was to have a light-hearted and chatty magazine programme to start the weekend. To get Michael Aspel, LWT had to buy his contract for commercials with London Transport.

'I wasn't allowed by the IBA to do a news and current affairs programme for LWT while at the same time doing ads for London Transport,' says Michael Aspel. 'So LWT bought me out. It was very flattering. When the first three pilots of the show were so unpromising and depressing, I was afraid LWT had made a terrible mistake.'

To start with, Michael did the show with Janet Street-Porter. Then Danny Baker came in. Despite the pilots, the team persisted and went on the air. To their relief the show seemed to capture the right mood and immediately became a popular curtain-raiser to the weekend.

'Perhaps we were lucky with the stories that first week. Anyway, the public took to it and there was a lot of laughter in the studio,' Michael remembers. 'It must have been the cheerful, offbeat mood of the show that made it work because we seemed to have the usual mixture of items you need for the weekend. It was very loose. We just walked into the studio and did it.'

In six and a half years there was a succession of female presenters. 'We had Janet, Paula Yates and Samantha Fox among them. We said that if Sam was going to come and do the programme we would never mention her obvious attributes. The only person who did – and often – was Sam herself! I always felt a bit like Perry Mason. Everyone else on the team was young and did most of the work. I did protest a bit about having to wear a tie when everyone else was in jeans and sitting comfortably. But ''managing director'' was my role.'

One of the show's many funny items was a talented pets competition. 'We had this whole team of proud owners and talented pets. After a rehearsal we sent them to their dressing-rooms and told them they would be on the air very soon. We did the item, awarded a prize, and all went up to the hospitality room for a drink. On the way back a researcher walking along the dressing-room area heard a voice of what seemed like an old man saying to his dog, ''Don't worry boy, they will be coming for us soon.'' He had never been called from his dressing-room – he could have been sitting there when we reported for next week's show. In the end we brought him back and gave him a spot of his own the next week. That's live television for you.'

REPORTING THE LONDON SCENE

The London Programme also gives local coverage to the more serious side of news and current affairs – a field of interest not always easy to pinpoint in a region where local and national issues are so intertwined. Because London is the capital and the centre of government,

The 6 O'Clock Show captured the right mood for a Friday evening. Its mix of light-hearted items and chat appealed to London viewers and it ran for six and a half years. Michael Aspel was the anchor and two of the regular presenters were Danny Baker and Samantha Fox

★

the law, finance and international communication, the stories and issues that emerge assume national importance more often than those in other regions – for example, inner city riots, disruptions in Fleet Street and the boom in the City.

Issues close to people's everyday lives are also covered – London's traffic, the shortage of housing for essential workers and nurses, litter, police stress, the Channel tunnel.

Trevor Phillips, a Londoner born and bred, has worked on *Skin* and *Black on Black*, and is presenter of *The London Programme* and a reporter on *Eyewitness*.

Trevor finds that being objective can be hard, especially which he is dealing with a harrowing subject such as a terrible disease or children in sad plights. 'The people concerned can't look at the item in the same way as everybody else. They may be aggrieved that you haven't covered some particular aspect that was important to them but not significant to the audience at large. You can see why they are upset but if you don't feel it is right for the programme, you can't do it. I do find those complaints most painful. I feel I've entered into a contract with the people to present their case fairly and if they aren't satisfied, it hurts that they feel betrayed.'

People with something to hide have learned a thing or two about intrepid television reporters, as Trevor has discovered. 'In the last series of *The London Programme* it was occasionally very embarrassing. We started to do a lot of "pursuit after villains" stories. Too often these people would open the door and say, "Oh, you're Trevor Phillips.

Come in and have a cup of tea,'' which can be a bit off-putting when you and your camera crew have gone determined to make the person come out and talk. That happened on a scandal where people were stealing from Brent Council and on a story about plastic surgery being botched. We went to doorstep someone concerned and when we got there he said, ''Hello, I know you. Why don't you come down to my country place and talk about things''.'

Some very serious stories are not without a touch of the ridiculous. When the famine stories started coming out of Africa and Michael Buerk had done his famous report for the BBC, Trevor was working on *Black on Black*. 'We decided to do a one-hour special and to include on-the-spot reports from Kenya where they had had months of drought. One

afternoon we arrived at this farm to speak to victims of the famine. The door of one hut opened and out came the fattest woman you have ever seen – the fattest famine victim in the world. She assured us she hadn't eaten in three days but she was hardly the right person to tell the story. We had to look elsewhere and eventually found people who really looked like famine victims in a setting of withering crops. They sit down outside a hut and I get ready, cameras are ready, and off I go. ''When was the last time you saw rain in your farm?'' One man opens his mouth and, just as he does, the heavens open and down comes the rain. It was the most ludicrous thing you ever saw. We didn't show that one.'

Another story that wasn't shown on *The London Programme* was when the team were filming for an item on rats

Shaw Taylor and *Police Five* continue to campaign and investigate getting the community more involved in combatting crime
★

infesting London. 'We filmed with an environmental health officer and we all agreed it was a terrible business and something must be done about it. As we were packing up, he suddenly seemed to realize what company we were from. ''Oh, now I know who you are! You're London Weekend! We are coming there tomorrow to get rid of all the mice in your kitchens''.'

Sometimes a story isn't pursued even that far but rejected from the outset. 'I let a big story get away in my *Black on Black* days,' Trevor is abashed to recall. 'A Nigerian minister, hounded out of his country after allegations of corruption, had come to London and rumour said there were hit squads after him. Someone offered me an interview with him for a five-figure sum. I said, ''Don't be ridiculous, we haven't got that kind of money to spend, and in any case who has ever heard of the bloke?'' He is public enemy number one, very important, I was told, but I still replied thanks but no thanks. Three weeks later every front page shouted the story of the Nigerian who had been abducted in a crate from London. Everybody wanted to interview him; nobody knew where he was. We could have made the money back a hundred times over by selling the interview – and I was the one who'd turned it down.'

●

POLITICIANS UNDER THE SPOTLIGHT

Probing the news and making the news – both have been the province of *Weekend World*. LWT's top current affairs programme, the one that has given it most clout, has offered the most serious analysis of what's going on. LWT only operates at the weekend when most people have their main leisure time. Making the viewers work to understand what is being said isn't a good idea. Nevertheless *Weekend World* ran for sixteen years, shown on Sunday at lunchtime. Its style and approach divided journalists throughout television and the press. Some said it was over-analytical and over-structured, dispassionate and boring. But the programme's advantage was that it had time to discuss an issue and interview politicians at length to get them to reveal something.

Barry Cox, Controller of Features and Current Affairs at LWT between 1982 and 1987, describes how the programme came into its own on major issues such as the Falklands War and the never-ending dilemma of Northern Ireland. Then it could put matters in some context for many viewers who came to issues only at time of crisis or tragedy. Even so, those who liked the programme did not claim to watch it every week. As with many current affairs programmes, viewers chose the issues and the people they were interested in most. *Weekend World* was popular in Fleet Street because it often provided stories for Monday morning.

The programme became an important ingredient in the weekly political agenda, helped by the stature of its presenters. The first, Peter Jay, was a journalist of considerable ability and influence who became the most important political interviewer on television. A former economics editor of *The Times*, he was not someone to be fobbed off with generalities or by devious politicians.

In 1977, after five years, he became British Ambassador to Washington, and he was succeeded on the programme by

Brian Walden. Jay was the public school son of a Labour Cabinet Minister. Walden was the son of a frequently unemployed glassworker whose mother died when he was young. A brilliant student at Oxford University, he became a Labour MP and one of the most articulate voices in the House of Commons.

Weekend World had been attracting about 750,000 viewers a week but in its later years it drew just over a million. Jay and Walden were different kinds of interviewers, although they had in common a determination 'to get a story' by using the research and the structure of the programme to its best advantage.

Brian Walden likes to plan carefully and the patient way he conducts interviews can be deceptive. 'You must ask some easy questions to which the person knows the answer,' he says. 'Let him hit a boundary or two, it puts him in a good mood and puts him off his guard.

'There is all the difference in the world between doing a three-minute insert into the news and having forty-

Mrs Thatcher is clearly the most significant British politician since Churchill, says Brian Walden. Interviewing her is always exciting and a challenge

★

LEFT

Brian Walden smiles a lot at the people he interviews. It is part of his strategy to get them to relax enough to say something revealing. Playing the harsh interrogator, he believes, can alienate the audience and make his guests dry up

★

Peter Jay, first presenter of *Weekend World* and the best political interviewer of his day before he accepted the job of British Ambassador to Washington

★

five minutes to question someone. An interview needs time to breathe – how do you establish anything when you only have three minutes? An interview is a completely different game.'

Brian Walden says that he has never been able to get critics of television to understand what interviewing is all about – they think it is some kind of confrontation, he says. 'But it's not about trying to trip them up or correct them when they have made mistakes in something – that's being smart. If you put the person off their stroke and they have been embarrassed by making a mistake, they won't have anything very much to say for the next ten minutes.'

If you notice, Brian Walden smiles a lot. 'All the stern-faced, prosecuting-counsel technique does is to make people freeze and reveal nothing. What it often does show is that such inter-viewers are even nastier than their guests. I am not there to show that I am cleverer than they are. I am there to get them to say something that matters to the public.'

Someone he found very difficult to interview was James Callaghan, the former Labour Prime Minister. 'But it depends on what you want. If you want an amiable, friendly chat with a few pomposities and a lot of generalities, there is nothing wrong with Jim at all. But if you want to get to the bottom of something, he is a very difficult chap to interview because he doesn't want to tell you.'

Miners' leader Arthur Scargill is the opposite, says Brian Walden. 'He tells you exactly what he thinks. He answers the question but answers about four others at the same time! You know where you are with Arthur.'

Among his favourites to interview are Denis Healey and John Biffen. 'With John Biffen it is the utter honesty of his answers. He will answer anything you ask him. He is superbly analytical and that makes him so pleasant and such an exception among politicians.

'Some people come across well when they have space to explain. John Biffen is certainly one; Enoch Powell does and in many ways Ted Heath does. He likes the opportunity to explain things and you will get a lot out of him. I always enjoy interviewing Nigel Lawson also – and getting headlines out of him.

'The whole knack of interviewing is to get politicians to say something that is really significant. Directly they realize what they are doing, they will shut up. Because they don't really want to explain what a problem is all about; that's too near the knuckle. A touch of light-heartedness distracts them from the gravity of what they are saying.'

Politicians do take more care with television then they used to. 'It's a mistake for them to think that just by appearing on television they will neces-sarily do themselves some good. My advice is that if they are being unfairly criticized, and are sure they are right, then they should think out their case and they will do well on television. Perhaps those viewers who didn't like them before may think again. If they haven't got a good case, my advice is not to try and bluff it out – that never works.'

The most momentous topic he covered was the Falklands War. The response the programme got to the coverage was more important than any other. 'The interview I did with John Nott, the Minister directly concerned, was very valuable. It was his very first on the Falklands. He had had a disastrous time on the Saturday in the House of

BROADENING THE CURRENT

To appeal to viewers, current affairs programmes use a wide variety of styles and employ presenters diverse in personality and approach. Because producers want to attract as many viewers as possible they regularly re-examine the ways current affairs programmes can be made and the performance and appeal of their presenters. Has a programme been the same too long? Do the viewers still like the faces they see on the screen as much as they did. These are the questions they ask. A key question for current affairs is, 'What should we be doing when the viewers see so much news?'

The question is all the more relevant today because current affairs programming will have to fight hard for its place in the schedules in future. ITV will have to compete not only with many satellite channels but with another ITV-type service in four years' time.

Television journalism is entering a new phase of increased competition for viewers – and there is enough competition already. Jane Hewland, LWT's Controller of Features and Current Affairs, believes that there is a bias in current affairs today and that it is important for the future to root it out.

'That bias is against popularity, a bias against the tastes, interests and aspirations of the ordinary people who ought to be our viewers. The people who oppose the popularizing of current affairs appear not to accept that factual television can have pulling power in its own right, uncorrupted by trickery or trash,' says Jane.

'Ordinary viewers are thought to have little or no interest in serious fact. The real audience for current affairs is assumed to be a much smaller group, often referred to by the programme-makers themselves as "opinion formers". I do not buy this division of the audience into an élite who want information and a mass who merely want entertainment,' says Jane.

Her guiding philosophy for LWT's new current affairs, locally and for the ITV network is that, 'generally the interests of our audience have been moving away from the public towards the private. The dramas that grip them are more personal and individual. They are more home and family centred, more oriented towards leisure, entertainment, lifestyle and possessions. But the problem is that traditional current affairs dismisses all these areas as "soft".'

Saturday has never been a day for current affairs but late on a Saturday night has been a place for 'infotainment'. The appeal of such a mixture of information and entertainment can be traced back to the BBC's success with *That Was The Week That Was* in the 60s. Ever since, many shows have tried to combine a provocative but lighthearted look at what's going on with sharp and irreverent humour. One of LWT's most successful ideas was *Saturday Night People* with Clive James, Janet Street-Porter and the late Russell Harty.

In 1987 Channel 4 launched a new 2-hour live programme on Sundays from 11.00 a.m. to 1 p.m. called Network 7. For too long the interests and tastes of young people were neglected by television and Channel 4 had set out to remedy that in its brief.

The new programme was an independent production for LWT created by Jane Hewland and Janet Street-Porter. Network 7 was fast, original in the way it used the camera and in its editing, and sought to convey information in a way that would attract young people. As the channel's Chief Executive, Jeremy Isaacs, pointed out, 'It did not rely on a bed of pop music for its appeal.'

It was presented by young people with little experience and perhaps because of that made the programme appeal to a young audience. It did interviews and features of all kinds, phone-in surveys and stripped information across the screen as an addition to what was being shown. One of its items that caused controversy was public readings from *Spycatcher*.

Clive James, Russell Harty and Janet Street-Porter livened up Saturday nights with their chats and guests in *Saturday Night People* (1979)

★

Commons (that was the only Saturday sitting of the Commons since World War II.). The nation was on the brink of being divided at a very vital moment. He had to be questioned in a way that brought out all the points he ought to have made the day before. He did well on the Sunday and I got everything out of him then that he should have said the day before.'

Chief headline hitters among Brian Walden's interviews have been those with Mrs Thatcher, including that where 'I listed a series of her attributes, of things she believed in and she agreed. And I said, but these are Victorian values. She said she very strongly believed in Victorian values and after that the phrase stuck to her. Mrs Thatcher is far and away the most significant politician since the war; that's what makes her very interesting.'

He is not sure that Mrs Thatcher is any different after appearing for ten years on television. 'Winning three elections and being PM for ten years has made her more confident, but I'm not sure her performance has improved. I'm not sure she is winning any popularity contest. I suspect that a lot of people at the end of an interview say, ''I don't like her but she looks as if she knows all about it''.'

Brian Walden now has a different series on the ITV network called The Walden Interview which is shown at Sunday lunchtime. Although his guests still include, politicians such as Nigel Lawson and Edwina Currie, he has widened the scope to include Princess Anne, Esther Rantzen, Sebastian Coe and other people in the public eye.

David Frost, one of the founders of LWT, was at the height of his popularity as an interviewer in the 1960s and 70s, being equally at home with major world politicians or people like the Beatles or American horror movie actor Vincent Price

★

'The *Weekend World* format was a multi-item format at the very beginning and in some ways you could argue that LWT's current affairs has come full circle,' says Simon Shaps, editor of the new Sunday current affairs magazine, *Eyewitness*, which has attracted 2 million viewers.

'The format that *Eyewitness* has adopted is similar though there are significant differences. We believe that one of the things that has made current affairs rather predictable in recent years was the absence of on-screen reporters.

'On-screen reporters are a cast of characters almost like a soap opera and they can lend an individual slant to the telling of stories,' says Simon.

Eyewitness is a more international show than *Weekend World* was in those early days. 'We have a person permanently based in New York and each week we do stories from many parts of the world. I think the world has moved on,' says Simon Shaps. 'People are used to seeing television of all kinds from all over the world every week. I don't think current affairs programmes should be any different.'

The change in union practices and the new technology has also made a difference. 'We can do what *Weekend World* was unable to do, which is to send one or two people to Brazil, for example, to do a complete story and use a local crew. We no longer have to meet the cost of sending many of our own people abroad to cover a story.

'Although Britain remains the most important part of our coverage, the public do expect their current affairs programmes to reflect the whole world,

not just Britain.'

However, one of *Eyewitness's* biggest scoops so far was in Britain. Earlier this year, in the wake of the Lockerbie disaster, one of its researchers got a job as a cleaner at Heathrow without any trouble and planted a package on a jumbo jet.

Simon Shaps says of his relatively inexperienced television reporters, 'You don't have to be a TV professional to appear on television. To some extent being a TV professional may make it rather difficult to be what we want our reporters to be – fresh, interesting and unfettered by the conventions of technology.

'We have to do three, four or five films every week but I think the format has justified that approach. If we get the balance of items right, we are unlike

anything else on British television.'

In addition to LWT's regular current affairs programmes there has been a continuous output of features and documentaries for local viewers, for the ITV network and for Channel 4. Series have included *Black on Black*, *Credo*, *Eastern Eye*, *The Law Machine*, *South of Watford* and *A Question of Sex*, and programmes have covered many subjects, among them unemployment, education, death, fitness, wealth, and – very controversially – a programme about the Resurrection, *Jesus The Evidence*. Various special programmes about or with members of the Royal Family have of course proved a major attraction, particularly *A Day In June* about the wedding of Charles and Diana.

The new Sunday lunchtime current affairs series, *Eyewitness*, has a completely different approach from *Weekend World* and is able to cover the international scene more. Its five reporters are Paul Ross, Jan Rowland, Michael Elliott, Trevor Phillips and Carson Black

★

PART FIVE

Stars with the precious gift of laughter

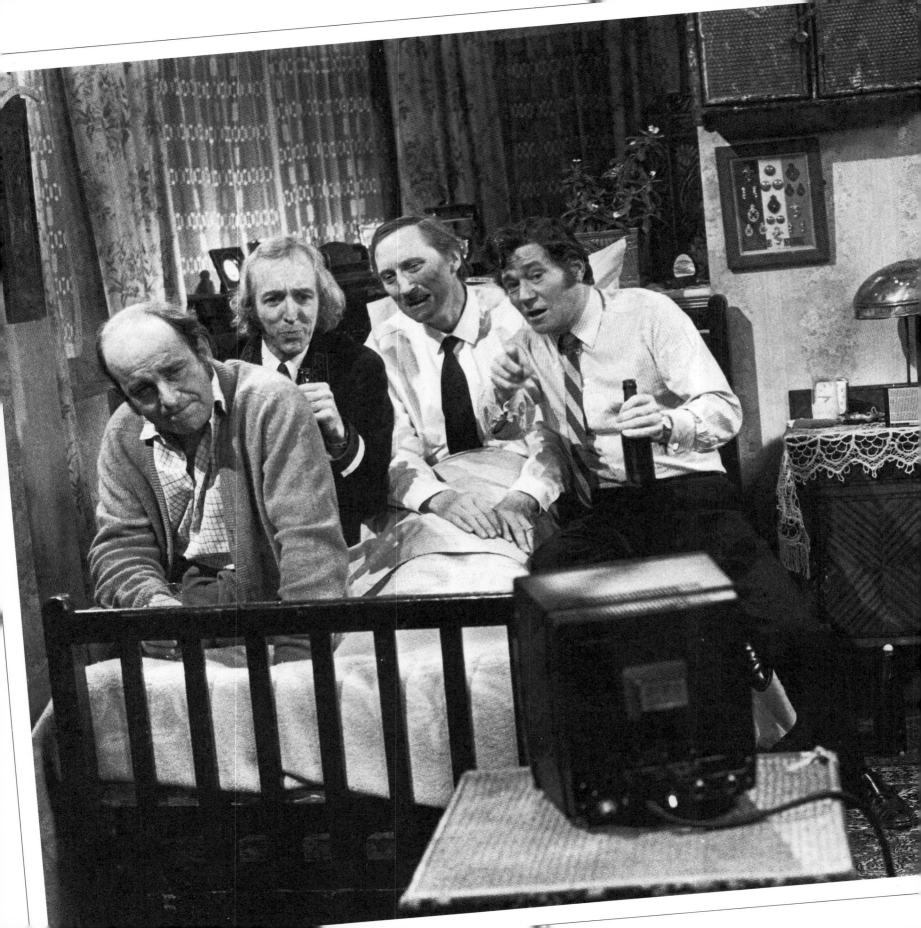

IT IS THE hardest area of television – and they call it light entertainment. It is about cheering people up, relaxing them and making them forget their troubles. But it is a difficult area because it involves taste so much. Not only that, but it can involve age, too – for example, the audience that likes Cannon and Ball may not like Ben Elton.

However, there are some shows that are hits because they touch a chord in all sections of the community. Situation comedy is the area you find that in most. But because there is such a voracious appetite for it, it becomes ever harder to satisfy the demands of quality and quantity.

Commercially, comedy at its best is a very desirable proposition because it can be repeated with great success – as viewing figures have shown.

Frank Muir had been working full time for the BBC and was head of comedy there, but he was not a BBC staff man – he worked on a freelance contract.

'After two and a half years of one three-year contract, I was wondering what to do next, when Michael Peacock approached me about a new company (LWT) applying for one of the ITV franchises that were to start in 1968. The BBC hadn't asked me to stay on (but they told me afterwards that they had all taken it for granted that I would).

'I liked the thought of starting something from scratch. It felt like drawing a raffle ticket for a Porsche. When my wife and I were driving back from seeing our son at Ampleforth we had the radio on and learnt that LWT had got the contract. We turned into a lay-by and shook with worry at the implications of it all.'

Frank was to be Head of Light Entertainment. 'We went in with a blank sheet of paper – simply aiming to make programmes that were successful and also worth making, which in comedy is quite difficult to do.

'We were all in one room just off Park Lane to start with and I remember saying to Humphrey Burton, who was in charge of arts and drama, "Would you kindly get your elbow out of the entertainment department." It was terribly cramped.

'I had a bit of luck because at the time the BBC turned down one or two things which the writers then brought to me. One of these was *Please Sir* with John Alderton.

'I had quite a lot of good shows. *The Complete and Utter History of Britain* by Michael Palin and Terry Jones was two years before Monty Python; it came straight to LWT. I had John Cleese and Graham Chapman writing the first episodes of *Doctor in the House*. That was brought to me by Richard Gordon, who is an old friend.

'I had my own show on the screen, *We Have Ways of Making You Laugh*. In it was a young American cartoonist called Terry Gilliam drawing during the first show. Unfortunately, someone had pulled the plugs on us because of a strike – the producer didn't tell us that we were blacked out. "Supposing the lights had come on again," he said. We went through it and it went well. But no one saw it.

LEFT

On the Buses was one of LWT's first major successes and it ran from 1969 to 1975. It had a cheerful touch of vulgarity allied to good characterization with Reg Varney (seen here with Michael Robbins, Bob Grant and Stephen Lewis) as the bus conductor who copes with his mates, his mum, homely sister and idle brother-in-law

★

John Alderton as the recently qualified teacher became somewhat harassed when he was sent to a tough comprehensive school in LWT's first big comedy success in 1968 *Please Sir*

★

'We had some good stuff in our comedy. Those were good days at LWT. We were all totally different individuals but we got on like a dream. I have particularly happy memories of the time when I was invited to lunch at Buckingham Palace for one of those meet-the-people Thursday lunches. I was desperately anxious to stop the department knowing about it – it seemed like such a grand thing to be doing. But I had boobed by getting my secretary to hire a car to come for me to make sure I would be there in good time. I got back to the studios about 3.30 and in between time the whole department had got to work in their lunchtime and sorted this out. When I came out of the lift there was a mauve crêpe paper carpet to my office and the whole of the entertainment unit were kneeling before me. They had made an orb and sceptre, and I was given a huge, wonderful piece of vellum with everybody's name on it commemorating the occasion. I have treasured photographs of that.'

The department's lively humour reflected that of the boss. 'Frank has a terrific sense of fun,' says John Alderton, star of LWT's early comedy success *Please Sir*. 'He used to do the warm-ups in the early days in the studio and he was very good at it.'

Please Sir was repeated from 1986 to 1988. When he knew LWT wanted to show it again, John asked to have a look at it first, because comedy doesn't always age well. He thought of a stringent test for it. 'I thought I would let the kids watch it – they had never heard of it. I watched them watching it, and they thought it was terrific, so I said OK after that. Children are a good barometer of what's funny.'

Although *Please Sir* had the authentic dingy look, almost the very smell, of an elderly school, it was all shot in the studio with one or two exterior shots. 'I modelled my role a bit on Donald Churchill who had done a schoolmaster rather well when we were working on a play together,' John says. 'I'd thought at the time I would ''steal'' that if the opportunity arose – it's what actors do. Donald was the writer of *Never A Cross Word*, which I did with Nyree Dawn Porter, where I played a Welsh student. It was because of that that Frank Muir decided to offer me *Please Sir*.'

Playing the caretaker in *Please Sir* was Deryck Guyler. 'He's a pure joy to work with,' says John. 'He is just one of the greats of recorded plays and comedy. He hasn't changed at all. And Joan Sanderson, who played the school administrator and teacher, is a wonderful comedienne. She was a rock, a solid rock of humour, as has been proved because she's just gone on into *Me & My Girl*, for example. I would work with her any time.

'I left *Please Sir* when I thought I had done enough – I usually do only one series of a comedy, as I did with *No, Honestly*. I like to leave when the series is at the top.'

Starring in *Me & My Girl* – with Joan Sanderson and Tim Brooke-Taylor – was Richard O'Sullivan. 'Ninety-nine per cent of the reason for *Me & My Girl* being a hit was the scripts,' says Richard, modestly. 'The writers gave us the scope for plots at the office, in the home and outside. With my ''daughter'' growing up, there was a wealth of possible storylines about adolescence. The series rested a lot on the daughter and Joanne Ridley was marvellous in it. If you haven't got a good script, you haven't got anything.

FROM SCRIPT TO SCREEN

How long does it take to make a comedy series? Humphrey Barclay produced many at LWT during his fourteen years there and is now a noted independent producer. 'Once all the scripts are assembled and you are ready to go, I would allow about eighteen weeks to do a series of six. But before that stage it will probably have taken three or four weeks for the writing of each single script.

'The six scripts will have had to satisfy the producer. The producer will choose a director (or direct himself) and the two will begin to cast the show, sometimes in consultation with the writer.

'When you have your cast, you will possibly read through the scripts – read them out loud – to see how they are sounding and use a stop-watch to check on the length. After a few adjustments, you go into rehearsal.

Judi Dench, the award-winning actress, had never been in a television comedy before. But when the producer decided to cast her husband, Michael Williams, in *A Fine Romance* he and the writer knew she would be ideal to play opposite him. So they asked her and she liked doing it so much she went into a second series

★

'The schedule will call for making one episode a week. The cast rehearse in a drill hall somewhere, then come into the studio for one day. They rehearse for the cameras, sound and lighting, then record the show in the evening in front of a studio audience. The next day is free.

'When you come out of the studio, you still have to edit the multi-camera video tape and usually tidy up the sound and put the music on.

'These days everything is totally costed, which means that you count the cost of everything, including the toilet paper! As an independent producer I can tell you that a half-hour situation comedy costs something like £130,000. When we were doing *Hark at Barker* with Ronnie Barker in 1970, I remember our budget was only £4,500 apart from the studio running costs.'

You might get away with a couple of weak ones but then the public would have found you out.'

Richard O'Sullivan was a big name by the time he starred in *Me & My Girl*, but at one time success seemed out of reach for him. He had been without work for some time when he went for an audition for the role of Dr Bingham in the long-running *Doctor* series. He got the part just for one episode, but he seemed to go down well and eventually became one of the regulars in three *Doctor* series.

Richard left LWT to go across the river and work for Thames in the hits *Man about the House* and *Robin's Nest* before Michael Grade brought him back for the adventure series *Dick Turpin*, made for a family audience. He spent a happy four years doing that but the

The excellent script for *Me and My Girl* led to some enjoyable exchanges between Tim Brooke-Taylor and Joan Sanderson: and Richard O'Sullivan and 'daughter' Joanne Ridley
★

change of style took some people by surprise at first. Richard remembers, 'After three weeks working on it, a prop man on *Dick Turpin* remarked how good I had been in all those *Doctor* series and other shows. Then he added regretfully, "But you're not so funny in this".'

Television series are an enjoyable medium to Richard. 'I like the way the work builds up,' he says. 'You begin with five or six characters, then the writers get more involved, the camera crew and sound men start, and by the end of the week you have about a hundred people all together on the same thing. It's essential that it is a good team with everyone getting on well together. In an ideal world you would have a day off after an episode is recorded, but in practice you start next day on the script of the next episode while the previous day's one is still in your mind.'

Richard thinks there is room for doing comedy both in the studio in front of an audience and on film outside without an audience. 'You can find it tough in the studio. The audience may sometimes need a lot of warming up if they have had a bad journey to get there on a rotten day. But you have to remember when you are recording that the people in the studio are just one audience. There are millions at home, relaxed and eager to be entertained. It's important to bear that in mind.'

Like many good actors Richard sometimes has his off days with the lines – which can be funny or make him a bit panicky. 'One week there was a line in the script that never seemed to come to me. But the director said not to worry, it would be all right on the day in the studio. When our studio day came I must have muffed it ten or twelve times and each time the director patiently said

TRY, TRY AGAIN

'My instinct about comedy is that script is all. That sounds rather pat but it is neglected at times,' says the man in charge of it all, Controller of Entertainment Marcus Plantin. 'Maybe we should be looking at some of the methods used in America to create successful mainstream situation comedy, such as *Cheers*, with very long legs.

'They use a totally different method from us, not our solo or duo enterprises but the team-writing concept. The team has principal writers, secondary writers and junior writers – the apprentice writers who get the rub-off from very skilled writers.

'American teams go for daily re-writes, hourly re-writes, last-minute re-writes. We get a script in draft, which is re-written and then stays more or less like that.

'A final script of one big American success, *Golden Girls*, is made up of a lot of different coloured pages, every colour denoting a different re-write stage. They record the same show twice, at five o'clock and again at seven and use the best takes. Very often they do a re-write between the two recordings.

'I am not saying that our best writers need that, but I think we might adopt some American habits. It brings on

young writing talent in a sheltered environment. Here the system is haphazard. You commission a writer and if it works, fine. If It doesn't, too bad.

'One snag for us at LWT is that our entertainment window is only at the weekend, the most competitive time. We can't have try-outs in "soft" slots. There is no soft slot at the weekend. It is a tough market, particularly for situation comedy, which does need to be allowed to grow. Few situation comedies take off in the first series.'

Nicholas Lyndhurst hit the jackpot with *The Two of Us*, starring with Janet Dibley, and over at the BBC with *Only Fools and Horses*
★

to the audience, ''Sorry, we'll have to take that again.'' By this time I was feeling a bit anxious but I finally got it right and the audience, who were really enjoying the struggle, clapped. The only problem was that it wasn't meant to be a funny line so we had to do it yet again because of the clapping in the wrong place.'

Richard's secret ambition is to become a director or get involved in some aspect of television production. Directing holds attractions for another top comedy star, Nicholas Lyndhurst. 'I thought when I was younger I wouldn't mind directing,' he says. 'I reckon I could do it but I would want a good few years more experience.' He's not short of experience now, despite his young and vulnerable appearance.

Before his two hit comedies, which were *The Two of Us* and *Only Fools and Horses*, he had done mostly drama –

Heidi, The Prince and The Pauper, Anne of Avonlea, and various *Plays for Today* where, he recalls, 'I played people who either got shot or blown up or I played policemen.

'I was first at London Weekend in 1977, helping to present a children's Saturday morning show called *Our Show*. It was pretty hectic for us. I think you could call it character-building. We didn't know from one minute to the next what would crop up.

'It was only really at the beginning of the 1980s that I started in comedy. That was a programme called *Going Straight*, a sequel to *Porridge*, where I played Ronnie Barker's son. My comedy hits have been great fun. There have been such lovely people to work with, very friendly and at the same time terribly efficient.

'Some people are actually convinced that I do live with my comedy partner,

A popular West End
favourite for many years –
particularly at the London
Palladium – Tommy Steele did
specials for LWT in 1972 and 73
★

Cannon and Ball,
two traditional music hall
comics who enjoyed a great
run on the ITV network from
1979 until 1988
★

Janet Dibley. They think that *The Two of Us* shows me in real life and that *Only Fools and Horses* shows me pretending. They actually compare the two – the series about my private life and the series with me acting. It's fine by me if they think that – very much a compliment.'

In real life, Nicholas lives by the sea. 'I am right by the beach so I can just go down to the bottom of the garden to do some surfing. I've been surfing for about five years. Apart from liking water sports, I'm passionately uninterested in sport.'

He does watch television, but as a pro. 'I actually enjoy watching comedy – but not just as a piece of entertainment like somebody who is not in the industry would. However hard I try not to, I am always considering the mistakes or how I would have done it, or things like that. I don't deliberately sit looking at the screen and picking a programme to pieces. It is a subconscious thing that a part of my brain can't help.' Which is his favourite comedy? 'If I were going to tape something it would be something like *Cheers*.'

Nicholas takes a very philosophical view of life and work. 'I really don't harbour very many ambitions, career-wise. I wonder what the success is going to lead to, but I am certainly not worried about it. There are various things I know I am not going to do. There are things it would be dangerous to do as far as type-casting is concerned. You have to take on new departures and risk people saying that they don't like you much in those roles. But you have to take the risk, unless you are perfectly happy to play the same character for the rest of your life – which I am not and I don't think many people are. Sometimes you

have to make a hard choice and decide, ''That's it! I'm not going to do anything like this again! I'll see what else turns up.'' The hard part is waiting to see what else turns up.

'I couldn't be unhappy or complain if my career folded tomorrow – I couldn't really complain about that because I have had such a charmed career to start with. I am a terribly lucky boy. Acting is a very dodgy profession at the best of times and light entertainment, especially, tends to use people up at a far greater rate of knots than drama ever would. I think everybody who reaches the top can save themselves a lot of disappointment and tension if they keep in mind that they have known far better days than most people in the country would ever dream of.'

Barry Took joined LWT in 1970 and took over comedy from Frank Muir who was one of several talented people to leave at the same time. Morale was a bit low when Frank left, but there was a legacy of such comedies as *Please Sir*, *On the Buses* and the *Doctor* series. Barry soon brought laughter back into the department and looks back on it as a happy time.

'I turned out to be a good administrator,' he says. 'We did about 300 shows a year and I saved ten per cent on budgets.'

Since he had come from the BBC he decided to have a word with a BBC producer friend, Michael Mills, so that LWT's hit comedy *Please Sir* would not be competing with the BBC's *Dad's Army*. The arrangement avoided depriving the public of one of the shows they enjoyed in their millions (remember there were no video recorders in those days).

'I think my most successful show was

Stewpot, with Ed Stewart. Children weren't being served on Saturday afternoons and I decided it should go out before the football results,' says Barry.

One little rumpus he remembers was over a guest spot on *The Simon Dee Show* in 1970. 'Simon wanted to interview the Archbishop of Canterbury on his Saturday night talk show. But I wondered if the Archbishop might end up going on between two semi-nude dancers and some musician who looked as if he was a pot smoker. Anyway, I had a quiet word with Lambeth Palace and Simon did a special with the Archbishop which went on in a suitable afternoon slot.'

Scripts crop up again as the core of comedy success when Humphrey Barclay reminisces about top shows he was responsible for. 'I prefer to start from a script. I remember when Bob Larbey was trying something different – he had always written with John Esmonde before; for example, *Please Sir* and *Now and Then* (1984). Bob wanted to do some writing on his own and came along with an idea that he hadn't written yet. He described the idea of *A Fine Romance* to me in about five sentences and I said yes.

'He came back with a great script and we started casting it. While I was reading it, the image of Michael Williams came into my head as the gardener. Bob said, ''Yes, great.'' Then we thought of the obvious partner for the romance – his wife, Judi Dench. She hadn't done a television comedy before, but we thought we'd ask her anyway to see what she said. The director was an award-winning drama director, James Cellan Jones, whom Judi knew well. She signed for six programmes. It was the only sitcom she had ever been offered

and she had such a nice time doing it that she was ready to do more.'

Another actress who is still very much a star today – Maureen Lipman – starred as an agony aunt with enough problems of her own in *Agony*.

'*Agony* was very difficult to do,' producer Humphrey Barclay remembers. 'The idea came from an untried writer, a Californian, who had sent a script to LWT on spec, about a Jewish mother running a sex shop. ''We can't use that,'' we said – but it was very good writing. So I asked the writer, Len Richmond, why he wrote it. ''My mother does run a sex shop,'' he said. I asked him if he had any other ideas and he said he wanted to write the story of an agony columnist with Anna Raeburn, the most prolific agony aunt of the day.

'It was a very long ride to get it onto the screen because it tackled very difficult subjects and talked grown-up language. It dealt with emotional and sexual problems. Maureen Lipman was brilliantly fraught and funny as the career woman harassed at work, by her Jewish mother and by her husband Laurence, played by Simon Williams. Two gay chaps next door were her best friends – and people liked them. They

Maureen Lipman as the fraught magazine agony aunt with her two gay friends, played by Peter Denyer and Jeremy Bulloch in *Agony* in 1979. It turned out to be a very difficult series to do – but the actress pulled out all the stops
★

Exploring new subject matter and styles for comedy has accelerated in recent years. 'We're always looking for fresh talent and ideas,' says Marcus Plantin, LWT's Controller of Entertainment.

A clear sign of this aim was LWT's signing of Victoria Wood to do a special programme, *An Audience with Victoria Wood* (winner of a BAFTA award). This went out as prime-time entertainment at nine at night. 'That's a significant change for ITV,' says Marcus. 'We will probably do more specials in that mould with major stars like Victoria.

'Such shows would once have been thought not suitable for mainstream television but we have recognized how the audience's taste and sophistication has been changing.

'Entertainment tastes go in cycles and at present we are in a cycle of situation comedy and broken comedy (sketches and links). We are certainly not in a cycle of music or old-fashioned variety shows. Our audiences like narrative. They like seeing ideas based on reality. They like wit and they also like the dangerous hint of topics that might be controversial,' says Marcus Plantin.

'The mid-1980s, taste for humour that was crueller and more violent – *The Young Ones* and Alexei Sayle, for example – is proving short-lived, but it cut a path for less unkind brands.'

weren't carrying the full weight of the show. It was the first time we were near getting a gay couple right.'

●

MAKING A 'DATE' WITH CILLA

'*Blind Date* is a director of programmes' dream,' says Marcus Plantin, LWT's Controller of Entertainment. 'No matter who we are, from grannies to kiddies right across the population, we are curious about our own kind and very curious about relationships. And relationships are *Blind Date*'s subject. But the key to making the programme a hit was the choice of host. Cilla Black was a guest on a Saturday night *Wogan Show* on the BBC (incidentally, the producer was Marcus Plantin) because she had an anniversary coming up. She hadn't been seen on television for some time. She brought the house down because she came across fresh and full of zest.' On Monday morning LWT producers David Bell and Alan Boyd, who had seen the show, were on the phone to her agent. They signed her up and they were certainly right. She proved to be good with contestants, witty and a great ad libber.

Alan Boyd, the producer who set it up, says, 'The show needs these qualities – and gives them wonderful scope. Cilla has made *Blind Date* into a family show in this country. Its set-up has dangers which have produced a sleazy show in some countries. We wouldn't have that in this country and the couples are carefully chaperoned all through their date.

'To get *Blind Date* on the screen took nine months' constant work from the time we started to the point it went

FAR LEFT
Victoria Wood's solo performance in *An Audience With Victoria Wood* was shown on the ITV network in peak time, which would have been unusual a few years ago but is a recognition that the ITV audience has more sophisticated tastes

★

Cilla Black makes *Blind Date* work as a very popular family show. It takes many months to set up a series and get the right kind of people. Cilla likes it when the camera red light goes on and she goes to work ad-libbing and making it all look easy

★

on air,' says Alan. 'The first year we did *Blind Date* 80,000 wrote in wanting to be on the show. When the public write in they are sent back a form asking for details about themselves and asking if they have been on a game show before. We try not to use people who have been on before. We ask what their hobbies are; what kind of shows they watch. We ask for a photograph and the researchers say whether it matches what we are looking for.

'For each series the producer and his team have to spend a long time going up and down the country finding the contestants. They would interview 500 to find one. It takes months and a great deal of research is needed before and after we find them.'

Cilla begins work at the studio stage. By then, she says, 'I have been given my potted version of all the biographies of the kids who are on the show. That's where my hardest work comes in, doing my swatting on them because I don't meet the kids until the show.

'I never really know what I am going to do – I don't have a script. I go on the studio floor and it all happens out there. It is very much an ad lib show.

'I call the candidates number 1, 2 and 3 to start with because I am dreadful at remembering names of people I haven't met. When I have met the person face to face it's different. I do actually meet the ''pickers'' who are going to choose dates because they get a bit nervous. They are all kept separate during the day. It's very much like MI5 on studio days.

'*Blind Date* is easy for me to do – I don't want to be flippant, but I do find it's not work for me; it's very easy.

'I love it when the contestants get on with each other but I don't like it when a boy is not very nice about a girl. I chip in and make that clear. I am very old-fashioned that way. I tend to be on the girl's side. Although I like them to get on, it could make boring television if they all said how wonderful the other was.'

How does she head off show-offs? 'I more or less say shut up. The great thing about coming from the north, where I come from, is that we can get away with being outspoken. People expect it. If there is a nicer way of saying ''Shut up'' I'll choose the nicer way, but the message is the same. They take it from me because I am from their parents' era. It's like accepting their mothers' authority at home. When one fellow was actually a bit cheeky, putting his hand too near my bum, I said, ''Do you mind! I've got a son who's older than you. Get off''.'

Cilla notices the differences between people from various parts of the country and confesses a great liking for the Belfast people and their accent, 'but they hardly ever get picked. Liverpool folk make good contestants, too. We've never had a boring scouser on the show yet! Newcastle people are great and Scottish people are terrific. The Glaswegians have similar humour to Liverpool people – although sometimes I can't understand what they are saying.'

Why do people of all generations and at all levels of society like *Blind Date*?

'You can sit at home and play the game with the contestants and get really involved. When the picker chooses the person you haven't chosen, you think, ''She/he is going to die when they see who it is.'' If the picker goes for your choice, then you think, ''That's good. Taste just like mine.'' The viewer is full of curiosity and suspense.'

Cilla says she cannot guess who is going to be chosen. 'Sometimes when they are not on camera the girl or the fellow will whisper in my ear "Tell me who to go for." I say, "I just can't." If I did, and they thought I had picked the wrong one, I would get the blame!'

She feels relaxed and free to be herself on the show now but it was different at the start. 'I remember when we were doing two pilots. It was like being in a nunnery. I was told, "Do this, don't let them do that! Don't kiss any of the contestants." I had a break after making one pilot and thought, "I'm not enjoying this; there are too many don'ts for me." My husband Bobby reassured me and told me to forget everything everybody said and go out and enjoy myself. I did and they never used anything from that first pilot.'

Surprise Surprise is very different. It's hard work for the producer, the team and the researchers – and very taxing for Cilla. Says Brian Wesley, producer of the programme, 'We could often research it for six months and track down a woman's long lost brother – and then the brother would say, "Well, I don't want to meet the woman," and that would be the end of six months' work. It is very tricky not to breach delicate feelings and taste.

'Sometimes the researchers start off with just a scrappy piece of paper – perhaps somebody during the war in Borneo met a chap in a field and would like to meet him again. It is a major research job. In the first series we had 300,000 letters from people wanting to find friends and relations. We don't go out looking for people. We only find people when relatives have written in.'

Cilla says it's hard work physically. 'For a start, the Cillagram, which people only see about two or three minutes of, can take two whole days' filming – and that's apart from the travelling. Then we have a script read-through and I have to remember all the names. I can't have them on an idiot board to read from because everyone would see that and I'm meant to be surprising somebody.

'Some of the stories are heartbreaking. It's emotionally draining to get involved in them, but I get those feelings out of the way before I go into the studio.

'There are ten shows in a series and each one takes me almost a whole week. If I'm lucky, I'll get Sunday off. On one of the days I am in the studio working out shots with actors playing all the people I have to surprise. The actors help me a lot because they have read the biogs, and when I ask them questions they can feed me back information which really helps me. We work until nine at night and I am back on the studio floor at eleven the next day after that rehearsal and spend the whole day doing the show. When it is over I go and meet the people I have surprised, have a drink with them and pose for photographs. The next day I am filming again.

'I am a bit worn out after a series but I get a lot of satisfaction out of *Surprise Surprise* because I feel I've done a service. We bring people together after so many years and they could not do it themselves.

'I can remember all the stories in all the six series I have done. I have lived with the story all week so I can pretty well control what I am feeling about heartbreaking stories but I always leave the shot after the reunion. I couldn't stay there – we have to supply paper hankies to the audience.'

On her days off Cilla is a telly addict.

Cilla Black and Bob Carolgees in festive mood while filming *Surprise Surprise*
★

He is funny to look
at and always seems to be
enjoying himself playing his
many characters. Russ Abbot's
style of comedy is simple and
obvious but it's 'being silly'
that endears him to the public
★

THE GREAT TV BOOK

Stanley Baxter
played more characters than
anyone else LWT employed.
Because of all his costume
changes his series took more
time to make than most. But
from 1973 to 1982 his shows
were always popular and were
recognized by many awards
★

She loves old black and white movies. 'I love a good cry; I'm a romantic. And I love cookery programmes – but I can't cook.' She is a fan of British comedy. '*Only Fools and Horses* has everything, and John Alderton is great – everything he touches turns to gold. I am keen to do a sitcom: a great script has been written for me for a series but I haven't got the time at the moment.

'For me the best television has to be real, it has to have heart, make me laugh and make me cry. Being a singer, I have had to show emotion and I love to do a live show because it is the nearest thing to a concert. I hate rehearsal. To get me going the red light has to be on.'

●

VARIETY TAKES A NEW TURN

Though it has died many deaths in the past twenty-one years, variety refuses to lie down. The name sounds old-fashioned but the idea of acts is very much alive. Some of the most popular entertainment on television has people like Dame Edna, Victoria Wood and Ben Elton going top of the bill and more often than not solo.

They are in the tradition of the greats of the music hall – but their 'hall' is the television studio and their audience many millions. They work for a sharp-witted, sophisticated audience with quick-fire, but strong, material and they are amazingly diverse and prolific.

Hale & Pace are a young double act in the great tradition of those who look as well as sound funny. There are plenty of young entertainers who get a chance on Channel 4 and want to follow them onto mainstream television.

Saturday Night Live **for Channel 4 gave young entertainers, like Ben Elton, a chance to get television experience**
★

'*Saturday Night Live* on Channel 4 was a great challenge,' says Alan Boyd, a former LWT Controller of Entertainment. 'On a Monday morning I would be sitting on the edge of my seat expecting to have to go to the IBA to get the belt for things we had done on the Saturday night – but that never quite happened.'

Alan Boyd's successor, Marcus Plantin, liked it as a training ground which brought on Ben Elton, Harry Enfield, Hale & Pace, and Fry and Lawrie. The young audience encourages these new entertainers and the older audience starts to see why.

One of the valuable things that television does is to show the public new young entertainers in talent shows. The performers get the chance to see themselves on screen and perfect their acts and producers can gauge the public reaction. Television can no longer jog along with the same stars never being challenged – there is too much competition between stations for that. The public do not want the same old faces doing the rounds of television shows as they did in the 1970s. But television has to be careful not to inject too much that is new too quickly.

Television has created its own variety on its own bill. And on that bill we have someone like Dame Edna Everage with a talk show parodying a talk show. That's the language television understands. The best performers have their own shows as platforms where they can display their talent at length; and the public who like it don't care if it is called variety, revue or whatever.

Now that they have their own shows, the best comedy talents don't need to perform in other people's. But on special occasions you can find them

Hale & Pace came from *Saturday Night Live* to the ITV network. They were chosen to represent ITV at this year's Golden Rose of Montreux and won the Golden Rose and the International Press Prize
★

Gloria Hunniford's
Sunday, Sunday chat show
features who's doing what in
the London region's
entertainment and interviews
British and international stars,
such as John Cleese
★

Bruce Forsyth can
hold a show and 'work' an
audience with his ad libs as
very few entertainers can do.
His current series *You Bet!*
with its variety of guests (here,
former Liberal Leader David
Steel) and challengers needs all
his know-how on the studio
floor
★

RIGHT

The blend of music
and light entertainment was
the particular attraction of the
Live from the Palladium series
★

Stars gather to
meet the Princess Royal after
another fund-raising
performance at the Palladium
★

jostling in the old-fashioned way. LWT has had its share of producing huge Royal Shows. These bring their own satisfaction and problems.

David Bell is a producer and director who worked on many major variety shows in the past twenty years. '*The Royal Variety Performance* is in November but you have to start early in the year setting it up,' says David. 'The first problem is getting the "Yes" from entertainers to appear. November is the time of year when many good artists are touring, particularly in America and Australia. It is high season for variety artists to earn money in places like Las Vegas.'

Having done so many Royal shows, LWT has built up a great deal of know-how about making them. All the production people know exactly what they are doing. 'The hardest thing to get right,' says David Bell, 'is what the public sees – the entertainment. It is a very public show and it only takes one top act to get it wrong or not do as well as we had hoped and it can spoil the show. It's different from doing a big show in the studio. *The Royal Variety Performance*, for example, is a vast bill and the dressing-rooms at the Palladium are not very big and it means putting major stars together who normally have their own dressing-rooms. A glass of champagne and a few flowers are useful in sorting out any problems,' says David. 'That show is on a Monday night and we would go in on the Wednesday before to set it up. We would then rehearse on Saturday, Sunday and on Monday.'

Apart from doing *The Royal Variety Performance*, David Bell has worked on *A Royal Night of a Hundred Stars* and *Actors' Equity's 50th Anniversary at the National Theatre*. Another show really stands out in his mind. 'The Falklands gala – *A National Salute* – was a marvellous evening at the Coliseum in 1982. We had won the fighting and the stars were out to say "thank you" to the troops. Laurence Olivier introduced the services one by one on stage. It was a great patriotic evening with everyone singing along with the stars like Vera Lynn, Tommy Steele, Roger Moore, Paul Daniels and Les Dawson.

'It was the most emotional evening I can remember. Prince Charles and Margaret Thatcher were in the audience. When the stars came on for the finale the reception was amazing.'

In the 1970s, two of the biggest draws in television variety were Stanley Baxter and Tommy Steele. 'Stanley's make-up took a long time so there would be two or three hours of waiting before he was ready for the next

GOOD SPORTS AND PRACTICAL JOKERS

They are vulgar and down-market to some, but millions of us can be involved, informed and diverted by them. Game shows of all kinds draw large audiences, although they are going out of fashion a little now as peak-time viewing. LWT produced some of the best until about two years ago but is now giving other ITV companies the field. It plans to make a series a year and experiment as it did with *Trick or Treat*.

Game for a Laugh (1981–5) was the company's most successful game show. Alan Boyd created it with Jeremy Fox, an independent producer. 'I wanted to make a real people show,' says Alan, 'mixing it with factual entertainment because I believed factual entertainment was the way forward for entertainment in the early 1980s.

'I created a format for an early Saturday evening show with a host meeting all the bizarre and unusual characters who abound in Britain. Then I met Jeremy Fox, who was working on an idea combining two American shows, *Truth or Consequences* – a stunt show – and *The People Show*, which was very similar to what I had invented. We put our ideas together and developed a show combining stunts and factual entertainment. We did a pilot and I chose four hosts – a practical joker, Jeremy Beadle; a journalist to interview the mad vicars, Henry Kelly; a very funny chap from *Punch-*

lines, Matthew Kelly; and a rose among the thorns, Sarah Kennedy, who came for her interview in a big floppy hat and is convinced that's why she got the job.

'Nobody was ever forced to come on *Game for a Laugh*. If someone vetoed showing their appearance once they had done it, we would go with their wishes. No one was put in danger on *Game for a Laugh* or confronted on camera with a situation where they couldn't say no. No one was embarrassed physically. Very few people turned out to be bad sports. But the skill was in knowing who to pick.

'Prizes for game shows are always bought at the going rate or wholesale. We didn't accept them if they were offered – which makers do as advertisement – because we have to be seen to be unbiased.

'We would never choose people who are out for a prize or are greedy. In fact, what people want most is a memento. On *Game for a Laugh* most people wanted the plastic brick it was acrylic and cost £100. They sat it on their mantelpiece so that when people came to their house they would say, "You were on *Game for a Laugh*. Tell me about it".'

Sarah Kennedy, Henry Kelly, Matthew Kelly and Jeremy Beadle were the first team for the very popular Saturday evening *Game For A Laugh*.

character,' says David Bell. It made the shows very expensive. Stanley played all the characters in a sketch so he had to go away and learn everything and work at getting the lines for every character into the right rhythm. Remember he was playing one character without the other being there, but when edited together it all had to have the rhythm of normal conversation or it wouldn't make dramatic sense.'

The *Live from* . . . series hosted by Jimmy Tarbuck, were the very opposite of the Stanley Baxter shows. They were real live shows and people wrote in to LWT for tickets. 'The very first one was a bit of a shock,' says David Bell, 'because we overran and were cut off. We were so used to editing studio shooting that we didn't time it properly. But it was marvellous to be live, to stand in the corner and know that the show was going out there and then.'

He looks back on the talent that LWT has fostered. 'We ''invented'' people. We ''invented'' Russ Abbot and Cannon and Ball. I made Russ go solo.

He was in a group when I told him he would never be a star unless he went solo. He agreed and he is.'

It wasn't just the stars David Bell enjoyed working with – it was the 'boss' too. 'Michael Grade was Director of Programmes and let you get on with it. He had enormous instinct for what was right and didn't interfere. He was thrilled when it was marvellous and if it was rotten he would back you up, which was great in an executive. You can't expect more in this business.'

●

COMIC CUTS – EIGHTIES STYLE

'I was shopping in a department store when the assistant recognized me from my show. She called over a manager who also said, ''Oh, you're Denis Norden, I know you. I love your programme.'' They chatted to me while I wrote out the cheque. When I gave it to the girl she said, ''Have you any proof of identity?'' Being a personality is one thing, but it's not good enough for a cheque. I still have to bring out a banker's card.'

Denis Norden enjoys the irony of celebrity and its limits. He has been celebrated for many years as a gifted scriptwriter but most recently as instigator and host of the hilarious *It'll Be Alright On The Night*.

'When we wanted to do the first one,' Denis says, 'nobody had ever heard of such a thing. The whole idea of giving us a television programme to fill with mistakes – other people's mistakes – was unthinkable. It required a lot of persuasion. The sources we went to first of all were the networks and the produc-

Stand up comedians were very popular in the television variety of the 1970s. Jimmy Tarbuck and Roy Walker, two of the best, are still popular
★

DAME EDNA HAS THE ANSWERS

One of entertainment's great character creations, brought into being by Barry Humphries, is Dame Edna Everage. She of the swooping voice, flamboyant outfits and domineering charm has captivated viewers.

Dame Edna herself says, 'It was a major step forward when London Weekend finally accepted my suggestion to do a talk show – they resisted the idea for some years but finally they did it as an experiment and I think were quite pleasantly surprised by the result.'

What are Dame Edna's own favourite programmes? 'I think she rather likes documentaries and women's programmes. She watches *Dallas*.'

When Dame Edna has to go out and meet her public how long does she take to get ready? 'Oh she just more or less goes as she is, you know. She occasionally has her hair done and things and goes to a little more trouble with her make-up now that she is a megastar, but otherwise her life is remarkably normal.'

What does Dame Edna think of Barry Humphries? 'I think she feels that he's tricked her contractually by insisting that Les Patterson appear on the stage shows as well and sometimes on a television programme. She doesn't get on with Sir Les and she feels that Barry Humphries, her manager, has let her down. At the moment there is no talk of change of management.'

Is Dame Edna keen on any hobbies? 'Well she still likes cooking. So all those cooking programmes she adores – those London Weekend cooking programmes! Cooking is still her favourite hobby. Thinking of others is her other hobby.'

Had Dame Edna not been a megastar what would she have been? 'I think she feels that she could have had another career as a writer. Dame Edna's life story will be published in October. It is by no means her first book. She has done a book of songs, a coffee table book and a bedside companion.'

Dame Edna (above) Joan Rivers, Demis Roussos and Jeffrey Archer and (below) someone equally as glamorous as the host Zsa Zsa Gabor

Child's Play, the quiz where panels of celebrities and members of the public tried to guess what young children were describing, was a real challenge to set up. It was a series that demanded a lot of time but in the end both the viewers and those involved fell for it.

Its host was Michael Aspel. 'After LWT mentioned *Child's Play* to me we looked at the American version because it is an American show. It was full of precocious four- to five-year-olds – very knowing creatures and a lot of noise and flashing lights and big money. I said, "No thank you." But the head of light entertainment, Alan Boyd, said, "That is not the way we are going to do it."

'What we did do was one of the most charming programmes I have ever been associated with,' Michael says. 'I thought it was delightful. People did try terribly hard to think of nasty things to say about it. Coy and faintly

sickening were the strongest comments they could bring themselves to make. I didn't have any such qualms. *Child's Play* wasn't a programme one had to apologize for because it was lovely. The only reason for discontinuing it was that I thought I had done enough and because it took so much time to make. The team were out lining it up for about ten months of the year. For every fifteen seconds of magic on the screen there were about three days of material you couldn't use.'

The man responsible for setting it up was Alan Boyd, who recalls, 'It was one of the most enjoyable shows to work on. We had to learn how to do it. The Americans gave the kids money for travelling to the studios in Los Angeles for the recording but we decided to go to the schools to see the children. I had done a show at

It looked like a simple show but *Child's Play* (1984–88) was a very time-consuming and at times stressful series to make. However, Michael Aspel, and everyone who worked on it, holds it in great affection

the BBC called *Rolf on Saturday* and I remembered that the best kids came from Wales and Newcastle. So we started by going first to Newcastle and school classrooms and sat on tiny little seats.

'In one classroom we asked the children to describe middle age and this little girl said, "You're not exactly young and you're not exactly old." Another one said, "It's when you go grey, when you go fat and when you go bald." At that point everyone burst out laughing.

'It was charming and wonderful to do,' says Alan, 'because such amazing things came out of it. Even so, some of the maddest stories in the department were about *Child's Play*. We reckoned that one of the producers found it such a wearing experience that he went round the world for six months to get over it.'

tion companies. We found the best way of getting material was to locate moles, as it were, in cutting rooms, editing suites and post production offices. They tipped us off about where we might find the kind of out-takes we wanted.

'Gradually, as the programme got better known, people started volunteering things. Then the idea was taken up in other countries. About twenty-one have their own version of it now and a kind of international currency has developed in out-takes, with its own rate of exchange.

'When a version of the programme was done in America, that opened a door through which we were able to give

them our out-takes in exchange for theirs. So it snowballed. As the number of sources grows, the choices become harder to make. Also, it becomes harder to find different clips now we have done the show for so long. We have sometimes used clips that were transmitted in programmes, but not often – mainly because of some quaint idea about not injuring our own – although some were so good that we fell for them. Most clips, though, are genuine out-takes that were meant to be transmitted, not bits from pilot or trial programmes,' says Denis.

'There are enormous problems in clearing the rights to the out-takes. LWT is most punctilious about this and pays everyone who appears in the out-takes – that's why you will notice we have very few which show an orchestra! When there's a shot of a singer, we tend to take the angle where you cannot see the backing group and cannot hear them either. Producers, directors and writers are paid, too, and the company that produces it, so it's not cheap.'

A major concern at the beginning was what showing their mistakes would do to people. 'We had a hunch that it would endear them to viewers, not damage or humiliate them,' says Denis Norden. 'And so it turned out. The laughter is always kind.

'The one who lent most support early on – even though the company he had worked for weren't keen on the idea – was Peter Sellers. Peter was an old friend of mine and said go ahead. Once he had permitted it, word got round and the bandwagon started.'

The most effective items come from dramatic situations or important occasions where dignitaries are involved. 'In other words the slip has to fracture the mood, as it were,' says Denis. 'Where the set-up is meant to be humorous anyway – an entertainment or a situation comedy for example – the slip is no so comical.

'We have a lot of out-takes that we can't show, though – of the Royal Family, for instance.

'*It'll Be Alright On The Night* has been exceptional to work on because you know that people are going to laugh. You know that you are going to cheer them up. It is just simply something that I knew would entertain people. I have no wish to try and reveal any insights into the human condition.'

The talk show is popular with audiences, particularly at the weekend. One of broadcasting's most engaging talkers, Frank Muir, was host on LWT's first chat show, *We Have Ways of Making You Laugh* (1968). The half-hour of wry observation got off to a poor start – it was blacked out because of a strike just as the new station was about to open. That was a bad omen for the show. It was considered too unappealing for the mass weekend audience and was allowed only a short life.

However, it did inspire a whole range of ideas and when the late Russell Harty eventually got his own show he became one of the popular chat show hosts of the 1970s. Clive James, who worked for LWT at the beginning, returned in 1979 with *Saturday Night People* and *A Question of Sex*. His witty turn of phrase ensured that for the next nine years his single programmes and *Clive James on Television* were some of the weekend's highlights.

Michael Aspel has brought a quiet skill to the talk show art which has made some major celebrities sound more interesting than they might otherwise have done. Gloria Hunniford's *Sunday Sunday* has demonstrated that women, too, can be successful talk show hosts.

Michael says his show, *Aspel & Company*, is recorded usually about two days before it is shown, which gives a day between to edit. 'We used to make it only a short time before transmission but these days we just let it roll. It sometimes takes people a while to loosen up.

'The guests don't get the questions in advance and I often don't meet them until we go on. I don't like to spend too much time in their company beforehand because it might spoil the mood. You could also get off on the wrong foot. I prefer to meet on the set, because then I

Denis Norden fronting *It'll Be Alright On The Night*. 'You know you are going to cheer up the viewers'
★

have some kind of status, I suppose the word is – it's my own place.

'I wasn't desperate to be a chat show host – it was just something I hadn't actually done. I had done most things from reading the news to doing *Crackerjack* for children. I just thought it was something I should try. I had done hundreds of interviews on radio and indeed on television but not on a bona fide chat show.'

What are the drawbacks of his job? Are there places he cannot go with his children, for example?

'I do my best to be just like everybody else. I am not going to let the job hamper me. If I want to take the kids somewhere they want to go, that's just what I do. I am often surprised when people come up to me in the street. I think they are going to ask me the way to somewhere. But in fact they are coming up to chat about the telly.

'I do find it more irksome than I used to. I get slightly irritated when something – an outing – is spoiled or I am trying to get into a taxi and someone I don't know wants me to stop and chat. I suppose as a young man you want to

Clive James face-to-face and eye-to-eye with Joan Collins
★

be recognized. It took a long time with me because I don't have the kind of face that registers.'

Has he acquired a way of fending off people? 'No, I usually just acquiesce.' Does he worry at all about how he looks on the screen or does he take himself for granted? 'I only worry that I have this unfortunate look of being very tired. I don't like to appear depraved – people might wonder what I've been up to. In fact, all I have probably been doing is playing with the kids and going to bed. I wish I didn't look so whacked all the time – it would be less of a challenge for the lighting men!'

What is his routine before he goes on camera? 'I have a shower in the morning and wash my hair. I go to the studios for a rehearsal, in slacks and sweater, and then go up to the hospitality room for an hour before we record, just to see who is around, finish notes and check with the autocue girl the roller for the introductions to the guests. Then I usually go down to the make-up room about half an hour before I go on, then back to the dressing-room to change.'

Has he thought out strategies in case things go wrong? 'I never have any ad libs ready. I have the formal introduction written out and hope that things will happen during the show that will give a chance to make it really good.

'We did have the famous occasion when someone well known appeared drunk. At first I felt concerned, but that was quickly followed by the realization that it was going to make good television. Unless, that is, it degenerated so much that it couldn't be broadcast. Such things don't worry me. It is waiting for things to go wrong that makes me sweat. When they go wrong, it's usually all right. The worst thing is that the

audience might get bored.'

He really enjoyed his special, *The Trouble with Michael Caine*. 'He is one of those people you know come through with the goods. It's almost a cliché that Michael Caine and chat shows go together. I am not the first broadcaster to thank him.

'The evening we had Margaret Thatcher and Barry Manilow on the show – separately – was fascinating. It was the first time the Prime Minister had done a TV chat show. And that's what we did, we talked about the life of Margaret Thatcher, not about life in the Conservative Party.

'I also had the rare experience of seeing the Prime Minister looking rather frightened. It was only for a fleeting moment backstage when I could see that she was clearly thinking to herself, "What have I got myself into?" The moment the music struck up and she was on she was totally in control.'

Does he find it difficult to concentrate sometimes because he is anticipating what his next question is going to be? 'You do have to concentrate. Television is not like radio inter-

Michael Aspel enjoying the company and varied views of Cliff Richard, Twiggy, Bob Carolgees and Spit
★

**Michael Aspel with
Joan Collins, one of his
favourite guests on
Aspel & Co.**

★

views where you can always go to a record or a commercial break to get you out of a situation. Television is much more relentless. All around you are people waving their arms or writing messages for you. But the rule is that you must always look your guests in the eye while they are speaking. You hope they will start by looking at the ceiling so that you can quickly look at what people are trying to tell you off the screen and then get quickly back. You mustn't be seen to be looking away from the guest in case they think it shows a lack of interest.'

Who would his dream show guests be? 'I suppose I would have the Queen swapping jokes with Frank Sinatra. But most people I would really like to talk to

are dead – great writers and great actors and comedians – Chaplin and Jack Benny would have been marvellous. Writers leave me in awe and I would probably do a poorer interview with the writers than with anybody else. And perhaps they wouldn't be sparkling conversationalists.

'It is quite sad to see people's reaction to very old stars who come on. The audience are quite often disgusted and will not forgive them for getting old. I once sat with the late Jessie Matthews in a studio watching one of her old films, *Evergreen*, and this wonderful-looking girl on the screen was terrific – but it was not the woman with me; she couldn't believe it was her.'